IVF'd

A Humorous Take on a Humbling Process

Jonathan Spradley

A special thanks for all you have done along the way.

Brandi Spradley

Mom and Dad

Dr. Kovac

Dr. Donahue

Nurse Kim

Kristie LaMantia

Jackie Grelle

To my wife,

When we said our vows and repeated the lines "for better or for worse" I had no real concept of what that truly meant. I knew it meant we needed to be there for each other in the good times and bad, but I never believed the bad times would come so early or last so long as we started our lives together. When I first married you, I loved you, but my love for you has grown and changed into something much deeper, more connected. Tragedy can do one of two things to a marriage, especially a young one; it can destroy it or forge an unbreakable bond. Fortunately, we have found ourselves in the latter.

You have lived your life with purpose and when you want something, you get it. Your passion for areas of interest and your ability to achieve great things inspires me. I have always admired your sense of humor and ability to take a joke. It helps me be who I am and has come in handy as we have faced life's trials. You ebb and flow with my strengths and weaknesses and have always been there when I felt I couldn't take much more. You provide balance and light to my life.

When we married, you were much softer than you are now; a softness that came from not being tested. By now, you have gone through fire, but anyone can go through fire. Going through fire is not the difficult part. Surviving, thriving, and making it through the other side stronger, wiser, braver, and more certain of yourself than ever before is a challenge most people cannot handle. You did. You conquered your fears and faced challenges you never thought possible. This process broke you, but instead of staying broken, you healed stronger than before.

Your persistence and tenacity have been incredible in the face of so many setbacks and heartaches. I thought I knew who I married, but you continue to surprise me at every turn. You carried on even when going no further was the easiest route. There were moments when I pushed and carried you, but there were many others in which you did the same for me. We were bound by marriage, but iron sharpens iron. We have faced one of the toughest challenges of our lives and come out on the other side more connected and more in love than ever before. I stand in awe of your ability to weather the storms that could have easily sunk us and know that we can face anything if we stand together.

Chapter 1

Nine months. That's how long they say it takes to have a baby. Just nine months. You're probably saying, "*It's technically closer to ten months... so...yeah*". *Ok, that's fine.* Ten months. Just ten months to have a baby. All of that is correct. From the moment of conception to birth it takes only nine, *er I mean*, ten months to have a baby.

In high school, the seemingly over the top hyperbolic message was, "Boys, don't get near a girl because you might get her pregnant by passing her in the hallway in between classes or gazing too sexily," and "Girls, don't look at boys because they are animals, and do you really want to raise a child all alone in a studio apartment turning tricks as a lot lizard in the parking lot of a Pilot?" As a teenager, the fear of God was instilled in us because it seemed that with any little slip-up, you were suddenly tied to someone for the rest of your life taking on a challenge you couldn't possibly survive. Essentially, your life would be over.

It is great to teach young people about safe sex, and maybe even instill a little bit of fear because I can imagine becoming pregnant in high school would be a life-altering moment. When your worries shift from, "How am I going to get this four-page paper done in time?" to "How am I going to raise a child?" it can be terrifying to say the least. The thing that is never accounted for, however, in the world of "ten months to have a baby" and "it's so easy to get pregnant so watch out" is infertility.

Infertility affects one in eight couples in the United States, and as much as having a baby in high school can rock your world, infertility shakes you to the core. Teen pregnancy is generally accidental and unplanned which creates shock and disbelief, but infertility runs deeper. Wanting to have a baby more than anything and then having that opportunity stripped from you is one of the most isolating, depressing, and all-consuming things anyone can face. Having something thrust upon you is difficult, but not being able to obtain something that can help complete your life? That's devastating.

The following story is simply that, a story---albeit a true one. You won't find many facts and you certainly won't find many hard figures. There are no real coping strategies or medically sound avenues for improving your chances. You certainly won't find a message that says, "It will all be all right," because how can I promise you that? I couldn't see my own future, so how could I possibly see yours? Some people face infertility, and everything works out in the end. Some face setback after tragedy after setback after tragedy and never quite come out the other side victorious. Part of "beating" infertility isn't just having a baby. Living triumphantly while infertile can take many forms such as living in the moment, not letting thoughts of having a baby become all-consuming, and finding a level of acceptance in the current situation and possible future.

The purpose of this book is to provide a real-life example of a couple facing infertility and how we got to where we are today. I promise to provide an honest look, a fair evaluation, and funny light-hearted moments that take some of the fear out of infertility and create little reasons for joy and laughter. If you want answers, you've come to the wrong place, but if you want a softer side of infertility to relate to, then here we go.

Chapter 2

In the summer of 2009, I was set to return for my junior year of college. I arrived on campus in mid-August, which was two weeks before classes started at Hanover College. Never heard of Hanover before? Don't feel too bad as plenty of people in the state of Indiana couldn't tell you where it is either.

Hanover College is located in Hanover, Indiana, and is an idyllic sprawling campus with around 1,200 students. A spacious campus must have room to exist which is why Hanover is located in a small country town with very little to do. Before a college student was old enough to visit the classically stereotypical small-town bar with two beers on tap and frozen pizza on the menu, the main reason for leaving campus was Taco Bell. This Taco Bell was such a draw for students that a sign was added at the edge of town promoting its location fifteen miles away.

I doubt I will get an endorsement deal for my glowing recommendation of campus life at Hanover College, so let's get back to what I was doing on campus two weeks before other students. The obvious answer would be that I was an athlete returning for training camp, perhaps I was the captain of the football or cross-country team. While I did run in high school, I did not have the athletic prowess to try my hand at collegiate sports. No, I wasn't there for sports; I was there as a Peer Advisor.

Hanover runs a different schedule than most colleges (I use the word college because it simply isn't big enough to be labeled as a university). You take four classes in the fall, four classes in the spring, and one class in May. While most of my friends from home were out on summer break at the beginning of May, I would still be in class.

While it was sometimes disappointing seeing my friends get together sans me, May term quickly turned into some of the best days of my life. One class for roughly two to four hours a day. That was it. My goal was always to take the easiest, shortest, and latest in the day class so there would be more time for hanging out, attending the month-long wiffle ball tournament, getting blitzed almost every night, and then having the one person who was sober---because they had been dumb enough to pick an 8:00 a.m. class---make the hour round trip into town for some of that heaven on Earth, Taco Bell.

To participate in this month-long state of bliss, Hanover students didn't start classes until Labor Day, and the two weeks prior were reserved for something called August Experience. I never attended school anywhere else, but it is my understanding that freshmen are usually dropped off on campus the weekend before classes start, receive a light orientation, and then are fed to the wolves. Hanover preferred an easing in approach to the whole "you now live in one room with a complete stranger whom you would've never associated with in a million years but is now sleeping below you, while a box fan in the window is your only source of air because air conditioning wasn't a thing in 2009 for some reason". Oh, and you have no friends. The only way to make them is to awkwardly stumble into a room where a group of people are playing cards who appear to have known each other for years and you're like, "That's not possible. How do they know each other? We just got here. How am I so far behind?"

I have lots of friends, but I have always struggled to meet new people because I am socially introverted at first. My mom sent me to at least one, if not two camps, each summer: soccer camp, zoo camp, camp at the YMCA, and on and on. I felt I always got there late after everyone had already paired off and didn't quite fit in. I hated it. I spent the first month and a half of my freshman year like it was a new camp, rarely leaving my room. I played hundreds of games of chess on the computer, watched *Family Guy*, and went to bed early. While it didn't work for me, August Experience was meant to help combat that very issue.

I was a Peer Advisor in the summer of '09, but it almost didn't happen. I had been an advisor the year before and had an incredible time. I met many other students and became friendly with people I would have never associated with otherwise. I had a wonderful group of freshmen to introduce to life at college and felt I had truly made a difference. I loved it so much that it was a natural assumption to go for the position again, and why not? I knew my group had given me a great review, and I had been on my best behavior. A week or so after my interview, I received my congratulatory email that I would be a Peer Advisor that next year, but there was one problem. It wasn't a congratulatory email; it was a rejection letter. They thanked me for my time but had decided not to bring me back. The competition had been fierce that year or something like that.

I was stunned. I thought I would be a shoo-in. As the shock wore off, indignation set in. Screw them. Who needs 'em? It was a dumb thing to do anyway. I am not very proud, however, so I quickly swallowed that feeling and followed up with an email asking why I had been rejected. The woman in charge told me to stop by her office which was located in a shell of a gym that used to be the pride of campus but was now a depressing space with offices scattered throughout.

The woman politely informed me that, "More candidates than last year applied, and the selection was very difficult this time around. Plus, you weren't the only one from last year who didn't get called back this year. We received reports that some advisors were drinking with their advisees."

I instantly turned red, feeling I was in trouble. "Ok, I get that, but that wasn't me. I didn't do that. Did my group report that?"

Her face got as red as mine had a second earlier as I had caught her attempting to link me to a dubious action and use it for some twisted example of justification. "Well of course not. Not about you…," she replied. "It didn't help that you weren't dressed up for the interview though," she quickly combated to regain the upper hand. "It appeared you didn't care."

Swallowing the irritation in my throat, I remarked, "*Ok*, but at least I didn't wear a hat this year."

"Yes, we remember that from last year," she said, as if it had left some sort of indelible mark on her soul.

"And if I didn't care, why would I be here now? Why would I have interviewed again, done a great job last year, and be in your office now? It seems pretty obvious to me that I do."

After the back and forth, I left with no expectations, not knowing if I had changed her mind or simply said my piece. A few days later, I got another email from her. My powers of persuasion had worked. I was the newest Peer Advisor for the next school year. Little did I know that one conversation would change my life forever.

Chapter 3

Our lives are pretty remarkable if we take a step back and examine how we got to where we are now. That is especially true when thinking about people finding love. I don't believe in soulmates. I can't believe in the concept that there is only one person out there for everyone. Nah, no way. Just one? I can't kid myself into thinking my personality is so unique that only one other person in this world can fit together with me *and* that one person has to come into my life at the right time and place. With the number of people who are married, to be that perfect of a system, it just doesn't make sense.

No, I don't believe in soulmates, but I do stand in awe of how if one event in the timeline changes, our lives could look completely different. That was the case when meeting my wife, who we will call Brandi to protect her identity. She too was selected to be a Peer Advisor in the summer of '09. She didn't have to fight to become one, though, because she is the perfect interviewee. She is articulate, expressive, and personable, which are all things I am still working on. I can also assume she wasn't wearing a hat, so there's that too.

The week before freshmen arrived, Brandi and I worked together in a large group but didn't interact much. It wasn't until students were on campus that I started to take notice. One of my tasks was to oversee a social mixer. The majority of advisors thought it would be a good idea to get drunk beforehand and show up at the event. The next day we were called to meet in the Science Center. Our faculty advisors had caught wind of the pre-social mixer debauchery and were incredibly upset. They asked me and a few others who did not participate in making a scene to leave the room while they talked to the rest of the group.

Um…let's talk about the irony here. They didn't want me to be a Peer Advisor because I wore a hat one year and didn't dress up, but here I was, a shining beacon of truth and light, being asked to leave the room because the rest of the group got drunk and made a ruckus at a school-sanctioned event. I'm not still upset about it or anything though…

That moment turned out to be the biggest, most life-changing break of my life. As the model citizens were gathering their belongings before the verbal tongue lashing of the year commenced, I glanced over in Brandi's direction and fell in love. Bending over to pick up her bags, I was left with a straight on, clear line of sight right down the front of her dress. A perfect line of cleavage separated two glowing, dancing breasts. It was love at first sight, or maybe it was just twenty-year-old lustfulness. Either way, I knew I wanted her. I didn't want her in some sort of sexual conquest way, but in a "I'm gonna make her mine" way.

As the small collection of the well behaved waited for the bloodbath to continue inside, our first real interaction was imminent, and I knew just what to do. I had taken a class with one of the other girls in the group, who also happened to be Brandi's sorority sister, and was semi-friendly with her. I used her as bait. I kept my focus and the conversation on her, virtually ignoring Brandi, and eventually asked her about coming over to my fraternity for a party.

"Why don't you ask me? I want to go to a party," Brandi asked, upset that she had been excluded from the conversation.

"Have you ever been to my fraternity? I bet you don't even know where it is. We aren't cool enough for you," I replied, further laying the groundwork.

"Yes, I do. You live over there. I would go there sometime, but no one ever invites me," she said nibbling at the tempting morsel of exclusion.

I knew this was the chance I was looking for to reel her in, so I closed, "Ok, fine. I'll tell you what. Next weekend, I will throw a Bill Cosby sweater and jello shot party, and you can all come. I personally invite you."

Two things here:

First thing: I was coy yet smart enough to not openly approach Brandi about coming to a party at a fraternity alone with a guy she didn't know at all. I relied on FOMO and safety in numbers, so she would feel comfortable committing while I weaved my master plan.

Second thing: My concept of a Bill Cosby party was way before I knew he was a monster, so lay off.

Bonus third thing: My first thing makes me sound like as much of a monster as Bill Cosby is.

I was well on my way to falling in love with Brandi and making her my wife, but there was one problem. She didn't love me back; at least not right away. Like water flowing over a rock, I slowly found the cracks and crevasses that I could sink into and chip away her defenses. Usually reserved for Sunday calls back home to my mom, I would furiously respond to Brandi's text messages with my flip phone. Punching the number "2" three times to make a C because I didn't understand T9, showed my true dedication to love. After much time, and a case of carpal tunnel from hours of texting but barely writing anything, water broke rock, and we were united.

I can't imagine that if Brandi was my only soulmate, she would have played so hard to get knowing the balance of the world and the fate of all lovers rested on that decision. I could have easily given up and moved on to the next girl whose chest caught a glimmer of the sun's rays. I could have given up when I had been denied the position as Peer Advisor and never sent the email asking why, but I persisted. That persistence had done me well in securing a beautiful, wonderful woman as a wife. Any persistence I thought I was capable of mustering before was about to be put to the test during the most challenging years of my life. If luck was going to keep its head buried in the sand, my old friend persistence was going to have to drag both of us through the next few years by the scruff of our necks.

Chapter 4

Brandi and I married in the Fall of 2015 and did what most married couples do. *No, we didn't bang all the time. Get your head out of the gutter.* We traveled, went out to dinner, hung out with friends, and just started to plan our lives together. We bought a house shortly after we were married because that is what married people are supposed to do for taxes, right? We followed all the steps to being a newly married couple. *What do you think came next? Yep, you guessed it, have a baby.* At first, Brandi wanted to wait because she "wanted a year to just be a couple" and focus on her career. *How romantic.* I was a little more impatient, but being the perfect husband I am, I relented and waited.

After a year of staying on birth control and not tracking cycles, ovulation, or anything like that, we felt prepared to go ahead and give it a try. Our maiden voyage was October of 2016, and we thought about how great it would be to have a baby the following August. Being deep into pregnancy in the middle of summer for someone like Brandi who already "ran hot" would be tough, but we couldn't expect everything to be perfect, could we? Well, October came and went, and Brandi got a call from her monthly visitor. Ok, so no baby on our first try. Oh well. We would just have the baby in September. That was as good a month as any other.

Months slowly started to pass, and Brandi became a little more tense after the fourth month. One evening in bed, I heard a deep exhale and could sense something was wrong by the way she was shifting and not finding a comfortable place to settle.

"Something isn't right," she said, turning to me with a glassy look in her eyes, trying to fight back the tears that were welling up inside.

Seeking to avoid a triggering moment, I responded encouragingly, "Oh come on, it has only been a few months. We just aren't timing it right. Let's do a little more homework (meaning mainly her). We will figure this out and have a baby by next year."

"I don't know. I'm not that sure. Most women are pregnant in the first six months, so the fact that we aren't yet has me concerned." Brandi knew the situation and her body much better than I did, and it frightened her. I wasn't scared, though. I was cocooned in my warm shell of ignorant bliss.

By the time the following October arrived, nerves were at a full tilt. Brandi had initially made a doctor's appointment for late August, but the fear was so powerful that she called and postponed it another six weeks. The thought that something could be wrong was so intense, she simply couldn't face it. That pissed me off because we had been trying for so long to have a baby. She finally had an appointment and canceled it because she was scared? I have since come a long way from that moment in regard to waiting on infertility, but at the time, it was unacceptable.

"Why did you cancel your appointment? That is another month or so we have to wait now," I asked, red in the face.

"I don't know. I just don't want to face it right now," Brandi replied in a sheepish way that quickly turned defiant.

It was one of those moments when the irrational thought process of "if I don't go to the appointment, then I can't get bad news, and if I can't get bad news then my worst thoughts can't be confirmed," takes over. The idea was if she continued to postpone, everything would remain the same, and we wouldn't have to deal with it.

Brandi moved past that moment and went to her appointment in October to meet with her hometown doctor. They reviewed her medical history, did bloodwork, and discussed her recent struggles with being unable to become pregnant. Another appointment soon followed with a different doctor, and the first advice she received was to lose ten pounds because it might jump-start her ovulation. Thanks, doc! After that frustrating advice, she was instructed to set up an ultrasound to make sure all the piping was in proper condition. *Don't you love it when female anatomy is referred to as plumbing fixtures?* The $800 ultrasound detected a cyst on her right ovary, which prompted a meltdown because that *must* be the reason we couldn't get pregnant. A second ultrasound was then ordered to see if the cyst had dissipated, and Brandi was referred to yet another OB-GYN for follow-up. After the cyst was found to only be a dominant follicle post-ovulation (I had help with this term!), the OB-GYN informed Brandi that cysts are quite common and that it was likely not the reason for our infertility.

Getting past that point and finding out the cyst wasn't impacting our success was certainly great news, but it also left more holes as to why we couldn't get pregnant. Before more tests could be ordered for Brandi, her primary doctor instructed her to have me come in for a semen analysis. They gave her a cup and brown paper sack on my behalf and requested I come to the clinic.

   I took off work early and went in for my analysis, which was incredibly embarrassing because not everyone was there for that same reason. I slinked into the overly bright waiting room, hoping to avoid detection, to find three people mindlessly flipping through magazines from two years prior and one woman staring up at the small corner television as if she had been forced into this action out of sheer boredom. It was all quite horrific to my male psyche as I stood there holding a brown paper bag like some weirdo bringing a sack lunch to the hospital, basically announcing I was there for a semen analysis.
I approached the front desk to explain why I was there. The middle-aged woman at the front, decked out in her brightly colored scrubs, was obviously at the end of her shift, as made evident by her slow call to action and less than welcoming demeanor. I stood there for at least thirty seconds before she barely lifted her eyes in my direction.

   "Can I help you?" she asked. Her tone was one of, "I should be friendly, but I am about ten minutes away from punching out. Let's make this quick". It was a tone I knew well, having spent my entire working life in sales and customer service. I used it myself when I was at the end of my rope but had to fake a smile so someone could feel good about buying a phone.

   "Yes," I replied, as if there was any other reason I was standing in front of her besides my need for assistance. "I need to do a semen analysis."

   The haggard lady instantly perked up upon hearing this news because she knew she could run out the clock. "Ok, but that won't be today. It's too late. The lab needs time to run the test and they won't be able to complete it. The sample has to be fresh."

Apparently, a sperm sample has to be fresh, like really fresh. Like farm-to-table fresh because it needs to stay warm. I essentially had thirty minutes to do the deed and get it into the hands of a highly trained "sperm-person". Since they were about to close up shop, that trip ended up being a bust. I was going on a work trip to Paris the next day and didn't have time to worry about it until I got back.

Returning from my trip, and with the embarrassment of my first failed visit still in my mind, I delayed my next analysis attempt. *Yes, I know I was previously upset with Brandi because she had delayed her appointment, but she was the problem and needed to get her stuff figured out, not me.* I scheduled my next appointment but ran into a tale as old as time that all men in their twenties face at one point or another in their lives; I couldn't find the brown paper sack that held my masturbation cup. *I know. It's so classic of a problem it's borderline cliché.* I tore my house and car apart looking for them because I deemed those items as essential to my appointment. I couldn't find the bag, and to this day, I have no idea where it is. Someday, somewhere, a brown sack containing a semen cup with my name on it is going to show up in the most unusual of places.

I went to the appointment empty-handed and luckily, they handed me a new cup and told me I could tickle my pickle at home which was a major relief. The thought of going into a room in which hundreds and maybe even thousands of dudes had "produced a sample" was more than I wanted to imagine. I completed the assignment in the privacy of my own home and immediately took it to the hospital, all the while keeping it pressed up against my body for warmth. I found it to be a strange and horrible world in which I had to look a stranger in the eye and hand them a bag of my semen. The indignity of it was staggering. After the drop-off, all I could do was wait for the results.

Chapter 5

Waiting for test results can be a very difficult thing to do, and that doctor's office sure didn't make it any easier. I enjoyed having to call them and then have Brandi call them after we didn't receive any results for a week. We weren't nervous about the results, but it was wasting our time when we could be checking me off the list and getting back to the root of the problem that was Brandi's body.

It was December, and I had just gotten off work. I was in the kitchen making a sandwich that I was preparing to grill to perfection on my George Foreman. I could just imagine the first bite into the warm crusty bread with the perfect amount of melted cheese hanging over the side with ham nestled inside. When Brandi got home, I instantly knew something wasn't right. She walked in the door and stood in the doorway. She wasn't close, but I could see the beginning of a smile. It wasn't a "honey I'm home" smile, though. It was a trembling smile that said I am about to explode but if I can smile for half a second, I might be able to control my emotions.

"What's wrong?" I asked, feeling I had no choice. I didn't want to know because I could instantly tell I wasn't going to like it.

"The doctor called with your results…and…it's zero," Brandi said in between sobs, barely able to maintain eye contact while she tried to wipe away tears that were falling faster than she could keep up.

"Huh, what do you mean zero? Like nothing?" I responded, putting the half-assembled sandwich down on the counter.

"Yes, like nothing," she continued, almost unable to finish the sentence. "They said the count is zero. Not low, but ZERO. How is that even possible?"

The trip my mind and body took from gearing up for a hot ham and cheese to hearing we may never have biological children was incredible. My stomach dropped and my heart stopped for a moment. I held her in my arms, and we cried. We cried standing up, then sitting on the couch, and finally lying in bed. I don't think Brandi had seen me cry up to that point, but I held nothing back. I remember both of us sitting on the couch holding each other and just letting it all out. We kept repeating the words "zero" and "how" in a sheer, doubting way. Everything was par for the course in our marriage up to that point, so how could this be happening?

Once the heaviest of the tears dried up, we started researching on Google, which is always a great idea and has never led emotionally vulnerable people astray. Surprisingly, it yielded a trove of useful information and even a glimmer of hope. Having no sperm is a condition called azoospermia which is a silly name for such a damning affliction. This condition can stem from various factors including genetics, hormonal imbalance, or a blockage. We were hopeful there was some sort of treatment plan we could follow, and our dreams could get back on track. We called our parents and informed them of the devastating news which was greeted with the expected level of shock, disbelief, and support parents should provide. We made the decision right then and there; infertility would not define or consume us. We were still Jon and Brandi with our own identity, and infertility was not going to become our albatross. We had planned that night to meet some friends for trivia, but instead of canceling, we put on a happy face and went. It was the only thing we knew to do.

Chapter 6

What do you do when plans change? Do you panic and spiral out of control, or do you remain calm, cool, and collected, ready to tackle the next thing that comes your way? Me, I panic. Whether it is cooking dinner and three things are done at the same time and Brandi has wandered off into the other room at the exact wrong moment, or on a road trip when we miss a turn and have to go a whole mile up the road and turn around. I even panic when someone says they are going to do something and then cancels at the last second leaving me to figure out a backup plan.

I have a routine, and I stick to it. I have a cup of coffee in the morning, a snack at 9:00 a.m., lunch at 11:30 a.m., one cup of coffee after lunch, and usually have dinner around 5:30 p.m. When I miss my coffee or snack, I get hangry.

I guess you could say infertility made me pretty hangry. Here I was thinking that we would have a baby, simple as pie, and everything would go according to my "schedule". I thought things would go so well that we would even have time to have a second, and if I could convince Brandi, a third. How wonderful it was all going to be. Infertility, however, threw my "schedule" so off track that it no longer made sense.

Instead of planning when I would have my three children, I was beginning to wonder if I would even have one.

Now, there is more to a family than having biological children. Some people don't have kids because they don't want any. They would rather spend their time doing things they want to do and not worrying about attending a parade of practices, recitals, or watching the same cartoon on a loop. Other people create their families in a much more blended style through adoption, foster care, sperm or egg donors, surrogates, and everything else in between. All of those are great ways to build a family, but that was not how we had desired to create our family. Our family was supposed to be comprised of little people who looked like us, spoke like us, laughed like us, and acted like us. *That seems much more narcissistic written down than it sounded in my head, but you get the idea.*

To many people, this idea of family is present in their heads for at least one moment of their lives. Some people are born knowing they want to be a foster parent or adopt, but for many, it is done out of circumstance or necessity. One thing I have heard a lot since joining the ranks of the infertile is, "There are so many kids out there who have been placed for adoption and need a family. Why don't you just adopt?" We thought about and discussed adoption, but it wasn't our first choice. Adoption isn't the responsibility of the infertile. We didn't feel that we were being selfish by wanting a child that is uniquely ours and comprised of a joint pairing of our DNA. That was how we wanted to make *our* family and it was *our* right to be able to pursue it.

Wow. I am a bit dizzy from being so high on my soapbox so let me take a step down. While I am prone to panicking at the unknown, Brandi thrives in chaos. She can hyperfocus when under pressure and do a lot of high-quality work in a short amount of time. The problem is that nothing has ever been hard for her. She was the top of her class in high school, got straight A's in college and grad school, married one of the most charming and charismatic men I know, and got the first job she ever applied for. A prospective employer even asked her if she thought the offered salary was high enough and whether they needed to increase it to compete with other offers. Meanwhile, I wasn't anything in high school, got some A's in college, didn't have the smarts for grad school, couldn't marry myself, and have been told I didn't get the job too many times to count.

Like I said, I panic, but I was made for the muck. Setbacks and disappointments don't get to me because I am a realist. I see the world as it is and understand that things don't always work out. Tell that to an optimist like Brandi and their heads will explode. That is how infertility got to Brandi. It's hard, and she isn't used to hard times. Not only is she not used to them, she is woefully unprepared to tackle them. I am not saying she isn't tough, but life has been relatively easy. When something comes out of thin air to punch her in the throat, it takes her longer to catch her breath. That is exactly why she knew so much sooner than me that something was wrong. It wasn't supposed to be like that. Everyone on Facebook seemed to be pregnant, and it appeared that every person on the street was carrying a bundle of joy. When getting pregnant is "easy" and it isn't easy for someone who is used to having success, that can gnaw at the soul. The most difficult aspect for Brandi was finding out the world had a nasty right hook and that it was time to take the gloves off to get what she wanted.

Chapter 7

After we gathered our mental footing, the next step was finding out where to go from there. I had no sperm but surely that wasn't the end of our quest, right? The next day or maybe the next day after that---I don't really know because after I found out I didn't have any sperm I didn't create a timeline in the off-chance I decided to turn this saga into a book---Brandi called the doctor's office looking for answers. Their suggestion was to set up an appointment with a urologist. A urologist? Aren't those for old people who are incontinent or something? I didn't know. The last time I had been to a doctor was for a sports physical in high school. I came to find that urologists are for more than just old people even though I was by far the youngest man in the waiting room by at least twenty years. I did get a little bit of my bravado back knowing I could fight anyone in the room and win.

It was late February, and the appointment had been made in December which helped teach us our very first important infertility lesson: infertility is a long, drawn-out process that requires a ton of waiting in between events. Patience is not a virtue either of us were blessed with, so this whole ordeal seemed destined to push us to the limits of what we could handle.

The day finally arrived for our first appointment. We walked into the incredibly tiny waiting room to find a literal knight decked out in a suit of armor inexplicably taking up precious floor space. There were only eight chairs, of which half were taken. The woman at the front desk must have taken the same training class as the woman at the hospital because although she looked at me right away, that is where the friendliness stopped. I was handed an iPad protected by an overly large blue bumper and asked to complete the standard doctor's office paperwork. I was initially encouraged to find only a half-full waiting room, believing it meant we would be seen quickly. The minutes dragged on as I tried to read a biography about George H. W. Bush but kept being sucked into the latest saga unfolding on *Dr. Phil* playing on the corner TV.

After more than an hour, we were finally called back to meet with the doctor and found ourselves in a room with wall-to-wall penises. There were posters on the wall chock-full of information regarding erectile dysfunction, a "How hard is hard enough?" display for which I apparently measured in at a three out of four according to Brandi (another shot to the ego), penile implants with little pumps to make your junk stand up, and everything in between. I felt out of place and nervous but knew I shouldn't draw judgment or make jokes because other people were facing obstacles and struggles just like me in their lives.

The doctor finally came into the room, essentially cracked his knuckles, and said, "Let's see what we got." We tried to tell him our story but like anyone who has heard it all, that information was not particularly useful when he could see, squeeze, and survey the area for himself. To engage his expertise, I rose to my feet and presented myself to the doctor in all my glory with Brandi looking lovingly at my backside. He gently squeezed, made barely audible grumbling noises, and then looked off into the distance as if he were attempting to recall the name of a song he couldn't quite remember. He said the veins looked fine but one of them could be a varicocele. To you novices with normal functioning penises, a varicocele is a vein that is enlarged which heats the sperm and kills them.

The doctor asked a few other questions, reached for his giant pad of paper, and began to scribble notes. He proceeded to tell us that one of three things could be happening: either there was no sperm at all, there was sperm but something was destroying it as it tried to escape, or there was a blockage.

Those were listed in order of worst to best-case scenario. I informed him that as a child I had hydrocele in which there was excess fluid on my testicles that needed to be surgically drained. My prior Google research had led me to believe that about two percent of babies who have this procedure will have issues with fertility later in life due to the development of scar tissue. That potential side effect was never mentioned to my parents, and while not everyone needs to be concerned about a two percent chance of developing life-altering, blindsiding, crippling infertility, it isn't completely useless information to acquire. If I had been privy to that information earlier in life, I might have had a semen analysis sooner than a year after trying to have a baby while shooting blanks.

The scar tissue that can develop from hydrocele surgery can close off the passage for sperm to be released. The doctor stated that was our best-case scenario and could ultimately be causing the issue. Tests were then ordered. He wanted me to do another semen analysis because their machine was more high-tech and spun the semen down to such a level that any present sperm would be more easily detectable. A blood draw was also ordered to test for a chromosomal abnormality that greatly affects your chance of reproducing. If that extra chromosome was present, that was it. No redoes. No checkpoints. Game over.

The second blood test was lower stakes, but it would gauge hormone levels. How was my testosterone? What were my estrogen levels? Why the hell would I have estrogen? Isn't that for women, women who are pregnant, nursing, or expecting to become pregnant? *Ok, that last part was more of a play on every medication commercial ever, but you get the point.* Estrogen? I already felt like less of a man and having to test my estrogen levels was a step in the wrong direction to regaining my manhood. Blood was drawn and sent to the lab for testing. Then we waited.

Chapter 8

Have you ever gone to a CVS or Walgreens and had to buy something a little bit embarrassing? Maybe you bought acne medication or hemorrhoid cream and had to look the person at the counter in the eye and hope they weren't paying attention to what they were ringing out. *Pro tip: Flip your items over with the barcode up. The cashier will think you worked in retail or are at least being helpful and you can try to pull a fast one.* Either way, my point is that it can be uncomfortable, and you can only "buy it for someone else" so many times. Thank God for self-scan checkout.

Now, imagine heading to a semen analysis and you have to tell a stranger you are there to masturbate. Well, that's what I did. The best part was I did it at the wrong office.

"Hello. How can I help you?" the woman at the front desk asked, smiling.

"I'm here for an 8:00 a.m. semen analysis," I responded, feeling my cheeks and ears turn red.

Ignoring my flushed appearance, she casually proceeded, "Oh, we don't do those here. That takes place on the second floor. Tell them you're there for an SA."

"Ok, thank you," I said, running from the room as quickly as possible to hide my embarrassment.

I found the elevator that took me to the second floor which looked completely abandoned. There was a desk with two chairs as I stepped off, but since no one was working the desk, I was unsure what to do. To the right was a large opening filled with empty cubicles and walls that had visible blank spaces as if something had been there but was no longer. It was as if the room had been repainted, but no one had bothered to move the furniture. To the left was a long narrow hallway from which a woman luckily emerged.

She turned the corner and eyed me like I wasn't where I was supposed to be. "Can I help you?"

"Yes, please. I need to do an SA," I said, unsure if "do an SA" was the right terminology.

"Oh of course," she replied as if this was the only reason someone would be on this post-apocalyptic floor. "Go down this hallway and ring the doorbell to let the lab know you are here."

No one had told me the jack-off room was on the second floor down a long corridor with a person that had to be summoned with one of those inside doorbell things. At the sound of the chime, a technician came from the back, and I explained why I was there. She came out from behind the desk and led me to an adjacent room. She pulled a plastic cup from her lab coat pocket and started writing my name on it.

"When was the last time you ejaculated?" she inquired, as if it were as common of a question as asking a person how they take their coffee.

"I responded, "Three days ago," but my embarrassment level was reaching new heights.

"There's a couch in the room, and you'll have one hour to complete this portion. No lubes, no oils, and when you are done, put the sample in this tray in the wall. Ring the bell again to let me know you are done, and I will come and get it. Sound good?"

The room was small, dark, and stank like ass. It didn't really stink though. That part is a lie. I can only hope it had been thoroughly sanitized after the last occupant, but I could just sense the stank that lived within the slick dark red couch positioned in the center of the room. Although it was cold, it gave me the same feeling of a warm toilet seat in a public bathroom. Knowing that a stranger had made themselves at home on this spot for a full hour, watching God knows what and doing exactly what I thought, was very disturbing. I had no choice as the couch and I soon became one. I took off my pants and underwear and created a picnic-style blanket to cover as much of the couch as possible before commencing.

Other than the couch, the room was empty. There was no television, no magazines, not even a sexy poster on the wall. I finished my assignment as quickly as possible, put my cup in the small box in the wall, and rang the employee again to inform her I was done. I kept my eyes on the floor and went back downstairs for my blood test. What a wonderful way to start a day.

Chapter 9

The results of the high-tech semen analysis came back before the blood tests. It took a few days and unfortunately, no amount of spinning my semen down could change the result. One hundred sperm? Fifty? One? Nope, not in the cards. After that, we anxiously awaited news of my hormone levels and the big kahuna, the chromosomal test. Those were some nerve-racking weeks, but the first piece of good news came our way showing that I had the necessary chromosomes to have children. That was a sigh of relief and although the dream still lived that we could have biological children, we knew it was a long road ahead with no real certainty of a positive outcome.

That April, an appointment had been set to review the bloodwork results and talk next steps. We arrived at the urologist's office, paid our customary "we will see you now" fee, and finally saw the doctor after what was close to an hour. My doctor took a minute to remember who we were and where we were on our journey before sharing the results of the hormone testing which confirmed close to nothing. My testosterone was slightly low, but everything else was in a suitable range for sperm production. The conclusion was what we suspected all along; my body was most likely producing sperm, but that same body wasn't allowing it to be released. A biopsy was suggested to see what was going on, to which we consented. After all, who were we to protest?

I had heard the word biopsy before on medical dramas but had usually heard it in the context of cancer as a way to determine whether something was malignant or benign. I wasn't exactly sure of its purpose or the required course of action for checking my testicles for sperm, but surgery is surgery. If the results of the chromosomal test weren't enough to make us flinch, waiting to have a surgery that would determine whether my body produced sperm was even more troubling.

The surgery was scheduled for May, and the best part was that it could be coded in a way that insurance would cover it. As most people battling infertility know, and particularly those in "red states", insurance and infertility don't mix. As soon as the words infertile, infertility, or broken penis show up on your insurance company's radar, you're screwed. Insurance companies will cling to that and associate everything you do with being infertile so they can find a way to deny you coverage.

My doctor was nice enough and smart enough and hated insurance companies enough to not fall into that trap. Since I had the hydrocele, which had most likely created scar tissue that was blocking the release of sperm, it wasn't difficult or misleading to code it under something, anything, other than infertility. The point I want to get across is that medical insurance companies are the devil and will do anything to suck the lifeblood from you for a buck. *As long as we understand that I can proceed.*

The operation was set for 8:00 a.m., but anyone who has had surgery knows that you can't show up on time or even thirty minutes before like at the doctor's office. No, for surgery we had to be there at least two hours early because I needed to get my wristband, complete the infectious disease blood test, wait in a big room, then be taken to a smaller room, get my IV, listen to a little girl scream because she had to get her fourth set of tubes, wait forty minutes for the anesthesiologist to arrive and talk about dripping medication through my veins, and then wait for the doctor to prep for surgery.

Finally, I was ready to be rolled back to the operating room. I knew everyone in the room was a medical professional and had seen everything before, but once again, I felt awkward. I knew that all those smiling people would soon be looking down the barrel of my most private area. Something about that didn't sit easy, but with no choice, I had to move forward and not think about it. Two minutes later, I drifted off to sleep as the anesthesiologist asked me a question I can't remember, and for which he certainly didn't care to know the answer. When I woke up, I found out if the dream lived on.

Chapter 10

I remember opening my eyes and seeing that I was in the same room as before. Brandi was standing by my side, and the nurse was at the foot of the bed. The first thing I remembered hearing was "They found sperm!" It was strange how such an underutilized, uncommon, and strange sentence could spark so much joy, but when I heard those words, a few tears streamed down my cheeks. There weren't as many tears as when I was told I had *no* sperm, but these were tears of joy. What did it matter anyway? I felt semi-emasculated by everything that had occurred up to that point, so it wasn't like crying was going to damage my reputation.

That is the thing about infertility though: I had been with Brandi for close to nine years, and I don't know if I had cried in front of her one time. She first met my family at my last remaining grandparent's funeral, which is a hell of a place to make a good first impression, and I didn't cry then. Now, with every turn in the road, I was tearing up to full-blown sobbing. What made the moment even more important and joyous was we had contacted a fertility clinic and arranged for them to freeze a sample of any sperm found. It cost around $700, which in all other aspects of my life I would have balked at spending $700 on much of anything, but in the world of infertility, anything under a thousand is a win. At that point in my life, I pretty much wiped my ass with hundred-dollar bills.

Like a jacked-up version of show and tell, the doctor came in to chat about what he found and had pictures of my little swimmers to show us. He had studied some under a microscope and found about two sperm per slide, which was considered a typical amount. They looked mature, like their daddy, and appeared to be in great shape. The fertility clinic was able to freeze three vials worth, and we were set. Well, kind of… we had the sperm but didn't quite know what the next steps were. Our doctor informed us that a follow-up appointment would occur in a month or so, and an additional surgery would most likely be necessary to repair whatever was causing the blockage. Finally! Progress.

So often with infertility, we either found ourselves going backward, or in an even better but still depressing scenario, nowhere at all. Wins were so hard to come by so we grasped at anything we could. Victories during the war against infertility are almost like stacking sandbags in the face of an approaching flood. You try to collect as many as possible, and even though you know that they can't stop all the bad from trickling through, you use them to buffer yourself when you can. Knowing I had sperm allowed us to build up some extra sandbags for the storm that continued to rage.

Chapter 11

One of the greatest factors muting the conversation surrounding infertility is male reluctance, especially if the man is the responsible party. Men are supposed to be strong, grow big beards, and spread their seed amongst any lady they choose. I won't go too far into the male psyche, but there is a direct link between a man and his penis. Self-worth can be felt in relation to size, function, and sexual drive that fuels a man's view of his masculinity. When the quality of sperm is poor, the quantity is low, or when there is no sperm at all, it can take a toll on a man's mindset.

When I first got the news that I had no sperm, I felt like less of a man. I had thoughts of not being able to provide for my family and believed I was no longer worthy of physical intimacy. Sounds silly but men are supposed to take care of things, ya know? When you can't perform a basic male function, it feels humiliating. The judgment, or notion of judgment, for most men can be too much. I am not saying that justifies male reluctance, but it certainly lends itself to one explanation.

When I received the diagnosis, my first thought was to research and see what could be done to correct it. Some men won't pursue any sort of treatment at all. No doctor's appointments. No pills. Absolutely no surgeries. Like I've said before, I was made for the muck. Maybe that was the difference. I am not saying I have low self-esteem, but I don't think *that* much of myself to believe I am above nature or won't accept the assistance of science. I didn't care to protect my ego because I didn't have one. Stubbornness and pride can get in the way of success and even cause some to never get out of first gear.

I can't say this as a statistically proven fact, but even when the issue isn't male factor infertility, men still seem more reluctant to hop on board with treatment. Is it because men tend to not care about having babies as much as women do? I don't know. I wanted to have a baby before Brandi did, so I doubt that is the reason. One thing I do know is that many children are conditioned and steered towards gender stereotypes starting with the toys they receive. Boys get race cars and balls to throw while girls get princess outfits and baby dolls to love. There is nothing wrong with giving a little girl a baby doll, but I do believe it drives a stronger connection to desire and care for something.

I have seen numerous clips of children being asked what they want to be when they grow up. When a little girl is asked, sometimes the answer is, "I wanna be a mommy." I have never seen a boy say, "I wanna be a daddy when I grow up." This does not apply to every single girl because many want to be astronauts, teachers, police officers, etc. No, not every girl wants to be a mommy when they grow up, but anytime a child talks about being a parent, they are usually a female. Maybe this feeling of being a parent is more inherent in females than males or just maybe this image is pushed on girls until it becomes a reality or expectation.

I am certainly no psychologist, and I am not trying to step on anyone's toes. I simply want to point out that good or bad, boys seem to be taught to care less about having a family of their own while a woman's "worth" is often directly defined by her ability to reproduce. That societal push for women towards desiring a family and children can create a stark line when involving the male in fertility treatments. The male may truly want children but does not possess the optimal drive to achieve success. The female may go to great lengths to accomplish this goal, but having a child always takes consenting sperm, and in many cases, consenting time, effort, and money. Brandi and I are usually on the same page about how we spend our resources but if one of us wasn't on board with fertility treatment, we would have either separated, or one of us would have most likely borne resentment for the rest of our lives.

I wish I had more suggestions on how to get your partner on the same page as you in regard to seeking fertility treatment, but I just don't have much to offer. I think they either will, or they won't. I like to think I bucked the traditional male role by being the first one to express the desire to have a baby. Additionally, I willingly sought medical advice and followed that by having surgery and taking multiple medications. Brandi took an interest but with a greater emphasis on the clinical side. She read more books, sought more advice, reviewed more studies, and went to more appointments. We both cared and equally desired success. Open communication and constant check-ins regarding where your spouse is mentally and emotionally is essential. Maybe being a male is a good enough excuse as to why some men don't seem to care as much. Then again, maybe it is just an excuse.

Chapter 12

The surgery was a success, and any future surgery would be at least three months out in order for my body to fully heal. Since the surgery was on the Thursday before Memorial Day weekend, I should have had more than enough time to rest.

Wrong. Brandi and I are fairly active people. I don't mean physically active like running or anything healthy like that but on-the-go active people. We are constantly attending events with friends, visiting family, and filling our social calendar. That weekend was no different as we had rented out our house for Airbnb. You see, in Indiana, Memorial Day weekend means Indy 500 weekend, and to Airbnb people around Indianapolis, that means payday. We had someone lined up to rent the house for four straight nights which was going to pay for our mortgage that month, and we couldn't pass it up. So, while Brandi had to mow (too much bouncing for me) I cleaned the kitchen and bathrooms. That weekend was usually our kick-off to Airbnb season, and while we prepared certain areas of the house beforehand, we couldn't do some of the more heavily trafficked areas until the last second.

I was a bit sore but feeling pretty good because the doctor prescribed Vicodin which is a crazy good drug. I am not encouraging drug use or wanting to make light of Vicodin because I know many people are battling opioid addiction, but *damn*, that is some good shit. When I was on it, I felt like I could be somebody, like I had the power to achieve my dreams. Everything came into focus and my life had new meaning. Not only were we preparing our house for Airbnb but since we couldn't be home over the weekend, we were also going on the Bourbon Trail in Kentucky. I was in charge of planning the route we would take, so I started mapping out the trip. I swear the Vicodin made me feel like I had unlocked some sort of secret route that no one else had found. The times matched up perfectly and the most beautiful route opened up before my eyes. I was invincible.

Ok, enough of my Vicodin testimonial and back to my recovery. When Brandi finished mowing, she found me on my hands and knees scrubbing spots off the kitchen floor. *Did I tell you how powerful Vicodin made me feel?* The worst part about cleaning was that we ran out of paper towels and had to get more. At this point it is important to note that the medical staff outfitted me in a loincloth type sling for my penis. Essentially, it was a speedo filled with gauze in which my testicles were chillin' like little eggs in a nest, quarantined from my penis with the latter sticking almost straight up into the air. Naked, I looked like a less visually stunning version of Tarzan.

Wearing gym shorts to keep the friction down, we headed for the hardware store. After perusing a few aisles, I caught a young girl, who was maybe ten, staring at me. Well, she wasn't so much as staring at me as she was at my junk. That sling had turned my penis into a compass pointing due north. I turned red, although not as crimson as she was, and turned away to help shield her from a life-defining moment that might require therapy. I went to grab the paper towels and saw the girl eyeballing my Tarzan-esque bulge again. I don't know how she was raised, but my mother told me to never stare twice at a man's surgically altered penis. I put the paper towels in front of me and then asked to push the cart for the rest of the trip.

Chapter 13

Not too long after we got married, we started fielding questions from friends and family, emphasis on family, about when the two of us were going to have kids. It was a fairly innocuous inquiry, but regardless of the situation, it was at best annoying and at worst, devastating. We have friends who have been married for years and don't have any kids. Maybe they have fertility issues, but most likely they just don't want kids right now. News flash: sometimes it's just that simple. Just because your grandma got married at seventeen and had her first baby at eighteen doesn't mean it's that way now.

Nowadays, women are more career-focused than ever and while staying at home and raising kids appeals to some, to others it doesn't. Qualifying for *16 and Pregnant* shouldn't be a badge of honor, but back then, things ran a little differently. The average age for a woman to have her first baby is mid-to-late twenties, and just because a woman is physically able to have kids before doesn't mean she is ready to or even wants kids. God forbid a woman who doesn't want kids or at least not right then, runs into one of those people that can hardly fathom the notion and says, "Well, you just don't know what you're missing. They are heaven's perfect little gift." Once again, to some people, children are the end all be all and to others, they aren't. We all want different things in life.

The biggest issue from my vantage point about saying things like that is that maybe the person you are speaking to wants children more than anything and is willing to have surgeries, pay thousands of dollars, and spend countless hours to have one and can't. The continuous pressure behind, "When are you going to have kids?" or "When are you going to start *your* family?" is like a loaded gun to a couple who is facing infertility. We wanted to scream and say, "Listen you asshole. We're trying." Sometimes we felt forced to play it off with a joke like "We enjoy having money," or "We don't know, probably soon," while smiling through clenched jaws, but what we really wanted to say was, "We don't know when. We are banging constantly at the exact right times of the month when ovulation is at its peak and are under so much pressure that sex is no longer fun because the thought of having to perform right then and there makes Jon go limp. Since we know we have to, he finds a way to eek some out, but then it doesn't work because he's empty down there and feels hollow inside because of it."

We can't say that though. We can't say that not because it isn't true but because Jack Nicholson's take on the truth was right. People want everything to be in cute little packages with tiny little bows and for everything to have a happy ending. Infertility ain't like that. Infertility is a smashed box on all four corners that leaks and smells rotten, and when you go to pick it up, your hand smooshes straight through it. People don't want that box. No, you either continue to spin the delaying and beautiful web of the "maybe someday" or "not right now" until you explode or do what we did. We told people our story.

Most close family members or friends are so in tune with your life that it is hard to shut them out of something so debilitating and constant. For the aunt we would see once a year at Christmas Eve dinner who would ask about children, we could brush off and just pray that next year we would be holding a baby we could hand off and let her change. Others in our life were simply around too much to ignore. It isn't even that we wanted to tell certain people in our lives, but when we heard the "When am I gonna have grandbabies?" question a hundred times, we reached a point where caving in was just easier.

Eventually, we sat our parents and Brandi's grandparents down and told them our story. We told them how we wanted kids, but it wasn't going our way. I am not saying every situation will be like this, but they listened and for the most part, backed off. We didn't continue getting those same questions every time we saw them, but instead, they either didn't ask anything at all or asked poignant questions about our journey. Don't get me wrong though. They still asked a lot of questions, but they were more caring or out of thoughtfulness as to where we were in the process and how we were doing. Sometimes the questions were still bothersome or painful to address, but we knew they were approaching things delicately and as best as they knew how. In the end, I am a private person, but it was freeing to let someone into my life.

My point is not how couples battling infertility need to buckle up and answer thousands of questions surrounding fertility and their quest to populate the Earth. My point is intended for those people who are asking the questions. Stop and think for a minute before you ask what seems like a relatively harmless question about babies. Maybe those people can't have children, like ever, or maybe they aren't far enough on their journey to know. Maybe the married couple is trying to lay the necessary groundwork so their marriage is strong enough to handle children. Others may be predisposed to certain medical conditions, and the thought of passing that on to their children is cause for pause. Finally, and the hardest for some to believe, is that maybe they don't want children. Some people enjoy spending their money on what they want, going wherever they want whenever they want, or simply find kids to be gross and annoying. Just because you have kids or had kids super easily when you "weren't even trying" or "by accident" doesn't mean it is a cakewalk for everyone else. So, before asking the inevitable question to a couple who has been married more than thirty-six hours, stop and consider this; they aren't you and quite frankly, may not want the same things you do in life.

Chapter 14

For couples going through infertility, life is full of ups and downs. Everything can appear to be trending in the right direction, and then, suddenly, the rug is pulled out from under them. With all the emotional turmoil, the infertile couple is not the only one who can find themselves on shaky ground. Family and friends can also find themselves navigating a minefield with no special equipment for identifying the trigger spots when trying to support those they love. As someone on the outside, they are not privy to every update and detail, and even if they are, they are still usually highly unsuited to provide adequate support. One wrong step and boom! Someone could explode.

As a couple who has called the world of infertility home, there are certain things we found helpful, not helpful, and sometimes downright damaging. Our thoughts will not apply to all people battling infertility as even Brandi and I have differing views of what was and wasn't helpful, but it should serve as a good place to start. If nothing else, it may act as a barometer when wanting to support but not knowing how or when.

Unhelpful: Tip #1: Providing advice

If your friend was attempting to open a restaurant, would you, as a fifth-grade English teacher, provide advice on where to buy commercial equipment, or how to keep books for managing expenses? What if your child was pursuing a doctorate in medicine? Would you provide advice as their father, who spent his life as a carpenter, regarding how to diagnose illnesses? I would hope not because how would you be qualified to offer advice on a topic for which you have no knowledge or prior experience? You could provide thoughts and suggestions but due to your limitations, those suggestions should be taken with a grain of salt.

The same rules apply to infertility. If a couple has a baby quickly and without any difficulty, how can they provide advice to a couple seeking treatment? They can't because they don't understand. Even those who have sought treatment should avoid providing advice when possible because not every journey is the same, and not everyone approaches it in the same manner.

The best thing people can do to be supportive is to listen without providing advice. We didn't want to hear, "If you just keep trying, things will work out." Will they? How do you know? How many years did you spend and what drugs did you take to have your first kid? "Make sure you are eating healthily and exercising so when the time is right, you'll give yourself the best chance to get pregnant." Oh yeah? Is that why women who engage in a plethora of activities such as drinking, smoking, and drugs still manage to get pregnant? Maybe they get their exercise by walking to the convenience store to get their Camels.

One of the worst pieces of advice that infertile couples are given is alternative options to having a family. "Why don't you think about adopting if you *really* want a family?" is a common topic that comes up.

Cool? Did you adopt? No? Is it because you had biological children of your own? That is bad advice on so many levels because first off, do you not think we knew adoption was an option and were choosing instead to seek treatment? An adopted child shouldn't be a consolation prize for a couple who spun the big wheel and came up short. It should be *the* option, the totally desired one. Whether someone decides to adopt, it shouldn't be pushed on the infertile as a fallback plan. We are not responsible for the existence of adoption and shouldn't be looked to as its solution.

Advice should be sought and asked for, not slipped into conversation, especially by someone with no qualifying credentials. Providing ill-timed, ill-placed, or ill-received advice can do much more harm than good to someone undergoing treatment. It appears you may be hearing but aren't listening. It tends to undermine or diminish feelings and thoughts by presenting a "simple solution" to a seemingly unsolvable and inescapable hell. A "Don't worry about it because…" or a "Well, why don't you…" paints infertility in a light of "No big deal" or "It's so easy if you…" but that is never the case.

Listening without offering advice demonstrates that you don't know what they are going through but still care deeply. You want to understand but you can't put yourself in their shoes. You want to help but might not know how. The reality is people going through infertility will usually tell you how you can help them through what may be the worst and most challenging part of their lives. You just have to listen.

Chapter 15

Recovery can be one of the biggest and most reoccurring aspects of infertility. In the case of surgery, my recovery was physical, but there was so much more mental recovery needed throughout the process. I believe that every person only has so much mental and emotional capital to spend at one time, and infertility comes around quite often to collect payment. I picture infertility as a gang of loan sharks trolling around to collect emotional payments. Gangsters jump out of a black SUV and proceed to beat the shit out of you every few months. Infertility shakes you down and keeps saying, "You got my emotional capital? You better have my emotional capital, or I'mma gonna bust your kneecaps." *Ok, so it doesn't sound as threatening when a gang demands emotional capital, but you get the idea.*

Post-surgery, in this case, was a more neutral feeling but with a lining of hope. We had found sperm and needed to wait until my body healed for an additional surgery that would attempt to repair whatever was causing the blockage. Technically, that wasn't our only option though. When we next met with our doctor, he explained that because the issue was from a blockage, we had two choices. We could either do a second surgery that would seek to repair the blockage or start IVF (in vitro fertilization). The idea was if we repaired the blockage, we would be able to have children naturally and the never-ending story would be over.

We had already put so much energy into an attempt to fix me that it didn't seem like we had two choices. We were both firmly in the second surgery camp. Brandi was in that camp because it wasn't going to be her balls ripped open for a second time and because it might spare her from the medication, side effects, and mood swings that accompany an IVF cycle. The longer we could keep the focus on me, the better in her eyes. That is a mean way to put it I guess, but she was right. If we could fix me and proceed as "normal" couples, then I was one hundred percent on board for surgery.

Chapter 16

The calendar slowly turned to August, and we were finally ready for the next surgery. *Remember how insurance companies are the devil?* Well, this surgery was another great example because this one wasn't going to be covered at all. I know nothing about medical coding, but it seems hospitals don't have enough ways to code procedures. My surgery was intended to fix a blockage that had resulted from a previous surgery. The only code that my surgery would fit under, however, is that of a "vasectomy reversal". It seemed a bit ironic because I imagine most men who have a vasectomy do so because they already have all the children they want, and the only way to prevent more is to collapse the mine. I clearly hadn't had a vasectomy, but there I was, about to go under the knife for a procedure that was going to be coded as a "vasectomy reversal". With that information, the insurance company started sniffing the air like a coon dog and picked up on the scent. I was now marked with a scarlet "I" for infertile, which is an impossible label to shake.

The out-of-pocket expense to have the second surgery was $7,200. We paid $4,600 in advance to the doctor's office, and the rest would go to the anesthesiologist and the hospital. To Brandi and me, that was a good chunk of change. We felt blessed to be in a position in life where we had the money to be able to proceed, but at the same time, it would have been great to spend that money on something else like a vacation or pretty much anything other than surgery.

We had friends who were pregnant at the time and the husband said, "Man, do you know how expensive having a baby can be?" He started talking about the doctor's appointments and the Lamaze classes, so I shook my head and asked, "You don't think I know how expensive having a baby can be? I have spent more money in the lead up to even having a baby." It was said in a joking manner, but I got my point across. Our hard-earned money was about to go to testicle repair surgery, and somebody wanted to talk to me about how expensive having a baby can be? Forgetaboutit.

Chapter 17

At 6:00 a.m. people exited their vehicles and began shuffling towards the hospital's front doors. We took the number "5" and waited our turn. After thirty minutes of listening to the muffled chatter of those being checked in before us, our number was called, and we proceeded to the front desk. We filled out forms and answered the clerk's questions. If you have ever had surgery, you probably remember they give you a wristband with your name, birth date, and other information on it. I assume this is to help them avoid the lawsuits that come from a patient requiring surgery on their foot and coming out with breast implants. I was about to receive my wristband when I was asked what should have been a routine enough question.

"I need to put your wristband on sir. Which side are you having surgery on?" the woman asked, rubbing sleep from her eyes.

Frozen with panic. "Um...which side?" I felt the blood bubbling up inside. It's my penis. It's both of my testicles. If it had been one or the other, well, that's easy, but when it's both, what do I say?

Brandi and I sat there looking at each other for what felt like an eternity when Brandi burst out laughing. I don't mean a giggle or when you are starting to laugh but try to keep it in by moving your mouth around or biting your lip. No, I mean a deep within the belly kind of laugh that the whole waiting room heard. As soon as she found a moment to breathe, she squeaked out the words, "in the middle."

With everyone red-faced, the woman checking us in actually read the chart and found the reason we were there that day. The nurse cleared her throat and said, "Oh, I didn't see what your surgery was for." She proceeded to wrap the band around my left wrist, and there was very little talking after that. Great start.

The second surgery took much longer than the first because it was an involved procedure, and the doctor ran into more issues than previously anticipated. The biopsy had only been done on the left side. That side showed scar tissue causing the blockage, and the thought was it could successfully be cleared out. All or at least most of it was removed, but there was still much more than expected. That caused delays and concerns that some might have been missed. The possibility that additional scar tissue would reform the blockage was another potential snare.

The right side was a different "ball" game because its issue sprang from a congenital abnormality of which we had no clue of its presence pre-surgery. In both cases, the tube had to be cut and reattached at a position farther up the line. The congenital side had to be moved up even further which was problematic. Just like an adult male who never leaves his parents' house and continues to live there well into his thirties, when sperm stay in the testicles and won't leave, they are not mature enough to adequately interact with a female. They need to continue to develop, and part of that maturation takes place in these tubes. The shorter the tube, the less developed they are, meaning the less mature they are, meaning the less adept at swimming they are. Just like Evil Knievel, sperm need a long enough track when attempting a death-defying feat. If that track is cut short, the likelihood of success is also cut short. In the end, the tubes were positioned further up than anticipated, and while that wasn't great, it didn't put a huge damper on the success rate of the surgery. Now my testicles sit up higher and tighter than before, so on a positive note, I essentially got a nut job for free.

Chapter 18

Fifty percent. That was the pre-surgery proposed success rate of what I like to call my "double nutectomy". Of course, many factors went into that success rate, but I truly felt that I had the advantage. I was young and wasn't attempting to reverse a vasectomy, so I felt my chances were pretty good. I also decided to play it smart that time around and actually rest.

I told you before they put me in a Tarzan style penis pouch to keep my Johnson off my testicles, but with this surgery, they added a very large bandage that covered the entirety of both incisions and everything in between. Have you ever removed a bandage from your testicles? I doubt it. I imagine you have removed a bandage from other areas, however, so you know how much those suckers can hurt. It pulls on the skin, and if it gets a hold of any hair? Well, that is some serious pain. People like to say, "Rip off the Band-Aid" when referring to a figurative "don't be a baby, and just go for it". It took me a minute to work up the courage, but once I did, I let it rip.

Immediately, I felt heat, which was quickly followed by that intense cold, clammy, sweaty feeling that proceeds passing out. While I didn't pass out, the moment brought me to my knees. My squeal prompted Brandi to ask (but certainly not get up because sound was an indication of life, and if I was still alive then it couldn't be that bad) what was happening.

"What are you doing? What's going on?" she asked in an annoyed tone as if I shouldn't be bothering her with something so trivial.

With a haze of blue and black dots flashing before my eyes, I proceeded to stagger my way out of the bathroom completely naked with a bandage half dangling from my pulsating and damaged scrotum into the living room where she was watching TV and collapsed onto the floor in agony. Gripping the edge of the couch, I whimpered, "I'm trying to get this bandage off but it's stuck. It hurts so bad." I felt so dizzy, like I was going to vomit. Heat then cold, followed by heat then cold and heat then cold. Back and forth with the room spinning around me, I felt like I was going to blackout.

While I was teetering on the edge and Brandi was laughing, she provided some advice. "Run some water over it," Brandi recommended.

"Huh?" I managed to say in between deeply labored breaths.

"Run some water over it to release the stickiness."

She picked me up and helped me limp over to the tub. From there I proceeded with such delicateness almost as if I was playing a high-risk version of *Operation* but instead of pulling a plastic Charlie horse out of a man with a red nose that buzzes at you if you get too close to the sides, I was peeling off a four-day-old bandage that had fused with the skin on my family jewels. It was sweet release when the grip let loose. I staggered over to the couch, and for the next hour, I struggled to recoup from my traumatic episode.

Chapter 19

Remember how the total cost of the entire procedure was $7,200? Well, when the woman at the urologist office was explaining the financial side of the surgery, I kept having her repeat the numbers because I hate it when my expectations are altered. Brandi thinks I'm rigid. I think of myself as regimented. *It all depends on how you look at a situation, right?*

I don't like it when someone tells me something and it changes. When we make plans and Brandi has an after-work event that suddenly pops up without warning, that irritates the shit out of me. She would point out that it has been on the calendar for a month, and while she is right about that, disregard that fact because I can't be held responsible for my actions.

Getting back to the cost of the procedure, the scheduler kept repeating the $7,200 total as a bundle. Their office would collect $4,600 upfront, the anesthesiologist would take $1,400, and the hospital would complete the total. The whole thing went sideways when we received an unexpected $350 bill from my doctor's office months later stating they had to perform an additional step which caused the total to change. I get that sometimes things don't go according to plan, but we were never told or asked for consent for this extra step. Would we have consented? Yeah duh, but that isn't the point. Have you ever gone out to eat, ordered something on the menu, and when the waiter brings the check, they state that the meal you ordered was heavier than expected so there is a seven percent upcharge? I didn't think so, especially when you had the menu in front of you and it said the exact price you would pay with no slick little asterisk to draw your eyes to a hidden fees and rules section designed to screw you.

The matter took several phone calls to clear up. It was very difficult to connect with those people because they worked regular business hours, and guess who else worked regular business hours? Me! I tried to find a few minutes I could slip away and prayed they weren't "experiencing longer than normal wait times". *For real though, if every time I called it was longer than normal wait times, then the long wait time was normal, and it had to be extremely long for it to be "longer than normal", right?* Once I finally got a hold of the scheduler, she couldn't make the decision to waive the extra charge but would be *sure* to speak to the doctor about it and get back to me.

Forty-eight hours passed with no return call. I spoke to her again, and she hadn't had a chance to speak to the doctor yet but had it on her list of things to do today. I love that line: "my list of things to do today". What that really meant was she hadn't talked to the doctor because she had lost her original note to do it and was actually thankful I called back. It still took a few calls, but my persistence finally paid off. The additional charge was dropped, and I was able to score one for the good guys.

The surprises didn't stop there though. Like a contestant on *The Price is Right* who didn't land on one dollar with their first spin, we hadn't maxed out on financial hardships, so we got another turn. The next bill was from the anesthesiologist, but instead of that predictable $1,400 amount we were promised, the statement showed a balance due of $2,400. I had several anxiety attacks during our journey where my heart raced, my head felt like it was whooshing back and forth against my skull, and my bowels raged out of control. I believe this event served as the kickoff. An extra grand on top of everything we had already spent was too much for me to handle. A surprise of this magnitude hit me like a ton of bricks.

I reached someone who explained that what was shown on the bill was accurate. About fifteen minutes into the call, I casually mentioned that the procedure wasn't being billed through insurance.

"Oh, so you're doing self-pay?" she inquired, as if this was the first time she had encountered a case of self-pay.

"Yes, I guess that is what it is called. Whatever it means when this is not being covered by my insurance," I replied, my tone starting to become irritated.

Failing to lead with this tidbit of news she then stated, "Oh, well, in that case, we can offer you a forty percent discount."

Elated, I said, "Ok, that would be great. So, the new total would be right around $1,400?"

At the mention of self-pay, a forty percent discount was now on the table? At no point during my conversation with my doctor's office was I instructed to call after I received the anesthesiologist's bill and simply explain I was doing self-pay to receive a discount. Was I the first person to have ever had surgery not covered by insurance? Was I stupid for not being aware? Does everyone already know this and is looking at me like well, yeah, you idiot? What if I hadn't called in to inquire about the bill and simply paid what was in front of me? What if I hadn't mentioned that I was paying out of pocket? That bit was organically produced over the span of a fifteen-minute conversation, not stated from the get-go. At the end of the call, I was certainly relieved, but not before I had a bad case of heartburn and an IBS flare-up.

The cherry on the proverbial sundae was the bill I received from the hospital. To their credit, the bill they sent was the exact charge I was expecting. The issue wasn't that bill, no, it was the second one that should have never come at all. When we were in the thick of surgeries and hospital visits, it seemed like the bills never stopped. We would be a month or two removed and then, like DJ Khaled says, "Another one." We couldn't stop wondering if we had already paid that one, if another one was trailing right behind, or if that was the last of them. The hospital didn't wait a month or two to release their bill though. It took them six months to send it. Six months to cut a bill for simple blood work. Practice makes perfect, so I did what I did best. I got on the phone.

I approach phone calls with companies the same way every time, with a kind but stern voice. People say, "you catch more flies with honey than vinegar", so I started with honey. The woman on the line proceeded to look at my statement, confirming the charges were correct. I didn't care for that answer, so I threw in a dash of vinegar.

"Do you usually cut bills for blood work six months after a procedure?" I jabbed.

I could sense the nervousness in her voice as she stumbled having been caught in a difficult position. "Well, uh, no. Not normally," she said, as she proceeded to put me on hold to check something which is code for "I just need to get off the phone for a second to gather my thoughts". "Sometimes the lab gets behind…Actually, that procedure was never run through insurance. Go ahead and ignore that statement because you will be receiving a new one shortly."

Getting my way, I switched back to honey and kindly thanked her for her help. I spent the next month waiting to receive an updated statement, and true to her word a new statement arrived. By that point, I had reached my limit. It was just like the rest of them; here is your bill. Now call us, wait on hold, and fight to pay the amount you truly owe.

Chapter 20

Have you ever been in a haze? Like one of those times that last maybe a few days, weeks, even months where you just don't feel like yourself? You tend to be more irritable than normal or lash out at people, and you simply don't know why. Maybe it is stress from work, relationship problems, or money issues, but whatever the case may be, you can't see the way out. That is how infertility feels. Infertility drained us of joy and energy and deprived us of wanting to do much of anything. We tended to get a lot of the "don't feel like it right nows" and the "I'm just going to lay on the couch and watch TV or scroll my phone because I can't use my brain for anything at the moment".

What's interesting is these feelings of blah weren't driven by major moments of catastrophe and sadness but instead by small happenings that continued to pile up. Dave Ramsey talks a lot about a debt snowball. Essentially, when trying to pay off debt, start with the smallest debt you owe and pay it off first regardless of interest rates. That creates momentum and allows you to continue to work towards your larger targets thus building a giant snowball or avalanche of success. Well, we were fully caught in the infertility avalanche of compounding effects. The small moments started to add up and multiply to create an avalanche that we couldn't quite dig ourselves out of.

When we were already down, smaller setbacks tended to feel greater than normal, and it took a more positive experience to outweigh them. During this trying time, Brandi and I each had a childhood friend die unexpectedly, my aunt passed away, and both of our pets died within three months of each other. Any one of those instances on their own would be burdensome enough to cause an elevated emotional response, but I felt those emotions could truly be processed and overcome. Our emotional groundwork throughout the infertility process was already fractured, so we had a more difficult time taking the hit. A sponge can only absorb so much liquid. Infertility is so much to take on that even small things such as a flat tire, an unexpected bill, or anything else that comes up can be difficult to manage.

Divorce is already very commonplace in society today, so it is not surprising to see couples divorce who are actively seeking or have gone through infertility treatment. Even though each spouse may ultimately want the same thing, having a baby through an expensive, scientific, and drawn-out process can take its toll. As I said, it takes a lot of energy and emotion, so there isn't always a lot of good mojo left to give your spouse. If both people aren't on the same page about equally wanting a baby, it can spell doom.

Brandi looked to support pages for solace and strength, but sometimes those places served the opposite function. The groups are mostly made up of women and some are not very happy with their husbands. Some women throw their husbands under the bus because he is the one with the issue, and it isn't fair that they have to take medicine and get stuck with needles. Others are mad because he isn't willing to go to the same lengths she is to have the baby. I know in other situations the roles are reversed, but the point remains the same. You can't row a boat towards a target when one person either isn't rowing, is rowing in the wrong direction, or has a broken paddle and can't help.

Ensure you and your partner are on the same page before starting infertility treatment. Perhaps you already have two children and one of you doesn't see the need for a third. Maybe one of you is ok committing to one cycle but can't agree on the financial aspect that accompanies multiple efforts. On top of that, it is becoming more and more important for couples to consider these types of things before they even get married. The vows we took said something about for better or worse. I don't remember the preacher saying, "And may the point come when conception is near and one of you cannot produce the seeds of life, you will still love and support each other." We certainly didn't fathom that "worse" would come within the first two years.

Infertility didn't come up during our marriage counseling sessions either. After a few months of counseling, our first minister refused to marry us due to me being Catholic and believing that I drank the Virgin Mary's tears for power or something like that. After being dumped for something I didn't even know was a thing, we met a new minister at Steak n' Shake. It took us a while to place our order as we got to know each other and discuss topics from his agenda. Once the food was on its way, I was hopeful that relief from hunger and the conversation would be near. Only my hunger relented, however, as we spent a total of three hours in that restaurant. Apart from being the longest any human has ever spent in a Steak n' Shake over the course of their lives, not one time did infertility come up. We were never asked what would happen if we couldn't have children. We were most likely asked about children and if we wanted them but never how we would react or handle a situation such as infertility.

Although it can be awkward, I believe it is important to have frank and honest discussions regarding infertility with your future spouse because it currently affects one in eight couples in the U.S. One in eight. That's a decent percent chance that makes it hard to ignore. Maybe the conversation doesn't involve the word "infertility" specifically, but perhaps the subject of "what if we can't have children" kicks off a dialogue? If having biological children is the only way someone will be happy in the relationship, it may be something to consider. If for some reason you can't have children, are you willing to sign up for an eternal grudge? That's your call, but at least you won't be blindsided.

The Handmaid's Tale centers around a world in which the number of fertile women declines, and the ones that are left are used as sex slaves with their sole purpose centering on giving birth to sustain humanity. While I know it is just a show, there may be more truth to that reality than some would like to admit. The fertility rate is on a downward spiral. Maybe women's bodies are evolving to not produce as many children, or maybe men aren't as manly as they used to be because instead of chopping down trees and plowing fields, we now sit behind desks and play video games. Either way, fertility is going in the wrong direction for people wanting to populate the Earth with their little clones, and if we are at one in eight couples now, where will we be in the next few generations? Sure, *The Handmaid's Tale* is fiction, but is infertility a concept that should be completely ignored?

Chapter 21

The second surgery was in August, and the next semen analysis was set for October. That was a little faster than the doctor would have normally ordered it, but I was going to Germany on a work trip and didn't want to wait. I wasn't sure if seminflukul analykukin was the right pronunciation, so I felt it would be better to be tested before leaving the States. There was a lot of nervous energy and excitement about finding out whether the test worked. We told ourselves no matter the results, we were going to enjoy our trip. Throughout the process, we tried to make a conscious effort to maintain as much normalcy in our lives as possible.

We were about two days out from the trip when we received the call with the results. *Any guesses? You're right! Zero.* We were disappointed but not overly surprised. We had kept that feeling of hope in the back of our minds even though we knew what the results would most likely be. We weren't discouraged because it was still very early in the process. A second test in December came a few days before Brandi's family Christmas party. At those parties everyone seemed to have a newborn baby, and everyone was interested when we would be having our own. At that point, we were praying for a Christmas miracle so we could have a positive experience to draw from that year. We thought we just might have a chance because about four months had passed since the reconstructive surgery.

Those results came back with a resounding…zero. With that fantastic news came the continuation of a new Christmas tradition for our not-so-fast-growing family. Some families have elf on the shelf or stringing popcorn on the tree whilst singing Christmas carols. Not in our jacked-up life. You see, our new tradition consisted of Brandi seeing a new baby, starting to look up at the ceiling while she fought back tears, and then proceeding to leave the party for the next forty-five minutes to go melt down in the bathroom, leaving me, a socially awkward weirdo to make small talk with her family that I see once a year. Yeah, I think three years in a row constituted being labeled as a tradition.

Chapter 22

It was interesting receiving my sperm count because of the way the information was transmitted. Of course, the doctor's office took their sweet time in reaching out with the results, so it fell to me to take the initiative. Once I finally got someone on the phone, the nurse always said the same thing.

As if it were his first day on the job and the document was upside down, the nurse said, "Well, um… well…huh…actually…it looks like you have zero…let me look at this again and make sure…Yeah…that appears to be right. Zero."

No one knows your situation as well as you do as the patient, but I felt like the fact that I was seeking treatment *because* I had zero sperm should have been highlighted at the top in bold letters with arrows pointing to it. For the nurse handling the file to be surprised that this could be the result seemed a bit much especially when I was hanging on to every word and hoping he simply misread my file. At the end of the day, nothing had changed, and it was starting to become our new reality as we continued to look for answers.

To make matters worse, I always had to receive devastating news in the middle of a workday. I usually had to call around one or two in the afternoon and then go back to work as if nothing had happened. That was hard to do. My life was being rocked and dreams were dashed but please, write this email about a trivial thing. Most of the time I would just sit at my desk and try not to think about it. On a few occasions, the anxiety would reach a fever pitch, and I simply had to clock out early and melt down on the drive home.

Chapter 23

After the first failed test, my doctor prescribed an anti-inflammatory to reduce the swelling from surgery because he believed it could be restricting the tube's pathway and reducing its output. The second drug he prescribed was Clomid. Clomid is usually prescribed to women to trick their bodies into doing what they should have been doing the whole time while trying to get pregnant, but in my case, it was recommended to increase sperm count. I got a thirty-day supply, and no matter how many times I got it filled, CVS always found a way to make the process difficult. After waiting ten minutes for one of the frantic employees to notice that a human being was standing at the counter, they would routinely tell me they didn't have the prescription, it was sent to a different pharmacy, or ask if I had received a text telling me it was ready while they scrambled to put together two or three pills to hold me over until they could fill the prescription.

Usually, when I got my Clomid filled (or not filled on numerous occasions) I would walk up to the pharmacy counter, the person would ask for my name, type it into the computer, hand me the pills, and ask if I have any questions. My favorite refill moment was when the young woman behind the counter asked me to say the name of the drug I was there to pick up when she couldn't find it in the system.

The young woman, seemingly fresh out of school, asked, "What are you trying to pick up?"

"It's called Clomid," I said in a barely audible whisper, hoping no one around me could hear the words coming out of my mouth.

Squinting at the screen through glasses that didn't have a strong enough prescription to see what was in front of her, she asked, "I'm sorry what is it?"

"It's called Clomid," I said a little louder but not too loud to avoid unwanted attention from the elderly lady taking her blood pressure with one of those do-it-yourself sleeves.

After a few minutes of awkward silence and searching on the computer, "Um…can you spell it for me?"

Stunned that I was being asked to spell my prescription out loud, I tersely spelled, "C.L.O.M.I.D."

I can't imagine making a patient shout and then spell the name of their prescription was taught at CVS technician school because it can be a private and sensitive moment to pick up a medication. Did anyone on my side of the counter truly know what Clomid was? I doubt it, but in my mind, *everyone* knew. Everyone knew, and everyone was judging me for it. "That guy is taking a lady drug" or "That guy can't make sperm," they would snicker and jeer.

This humiliation brought me back to kindergarten when I won a fundraising contest in which the prize was a limousine ride and lunch at Don Mattingly's (a local restaurant for our hometown hero) with the other top-selling students. I was looking dapper in my Mickey sweater and was feeling like a boss. My hamburger was a bit overdone, but I was getting to ride in a limo. I was riding high. On top of that, it was going to be featured on the news that night, so the day would live forever as one of two videos my parents would record of me as a child.

That perfect day turned sour when, on the way back from lunch, a girl in my class kissed me on the cheek. There were immediate oohs and ahhs from the upperclassmen in the limo, as they began to tease me. Being six, I didn't have the willpower to keep it in, so I cried the whole way back to school. Since I was no longer six, I knew I had to ride out the wave of embarrassment after chanting C.LO.M.I.D. and hope the pharmacist would just fill my damn prescription so I could go home. Whether my fellow pill poppers knew what I was taking or not, it was a perfect example of how one must get accustomed to embarrassment and shame while on this journey.

Chapter 24

While the Clomid settled in my system, another semen analysis was scheduled for March. We knew there was no hope left in my metaphorical tank and the March appointment would be the death knell for correcting me. Because of that we started looking down the IVF path. The obvious choice was to explore the fertility clinic currently storing my frozen samples from the biopsy. We hesitated, however, because not all fertility clinics are created equal. Just like with many for-profit businesses looking to sell you something, some organizations center around high-pressure sales mixed with fear techniques to make you cave, while others still want to make money, but do it the right way. The second type of clinic will work with you and listen to your concerns. They make suggestions based on what is best for the patient, not just their pocketbook.

The clinic keeping my sample, let's call them FarEast, was of the high-pressure variety; the type of clinic that understands FOMO and wants you to get every possible type of test for your body, your embryos, and every person you have ever met. Going through infertility can be a very long process filled with many disappointments and setbacks. FarEast understands these fears and preys on the fact that emotions can be a strong driver for many decisions.

People are trying to accomplish something outside of their natural ability that they desperately want, and a clinic is telling them to do a myriad of tests or success will be greatly reduced. If you want something bad enough, are you willing to risk going against the advice of your doctors even if it doesn't seem like the best thing for you? Can you live with the potential regret that accompanies passing on what is a "highly recommended" procedure? There is enough natural pressure that comes with infertility, so we turned away from FarEast and headed west.

Chapter 25

We started down the road to IVF but took an immediate detour when we decided to explore a clinic that implemented a newer and more affordable procedure, in addition to IVF, called INVOcell. Most stages of INVOcell treatment are the exact same as in IVF. Women take stimulation medicine to produce multiple eggs and then those eggs are retrieved. In traditional IVF, the sperm is then placed in a petri dish with the eggs for fertilization. The petri dish becomes a quasi-medical version of a teen sock hop where only the most perfect and prettiest eggs get asked to dance by the slicked-back-haired and smoothest-moving sperm. The egg with one eye that is smaller than the other and the sperm with gimpy legs don't get to dance and are left to die. INVOcell follows the same path up to the point of the sperm and egg social mixer, but instead of being placed in a petri dish, they are placed in the INVOcell device.

To increase chances of fertilization, rather than relying on the leather-jacketed sperm to mingle on their own with the poodle-skirt-clad eggs, you can elect to inject the sperm directly into the egg via ICSI (ick-sy) which is much easier to say than Intracytoplasmic Sperm Injection. One of the benefits is that sperm motility and count don't matter in this instance. When pregnancy naturally occurs, the sperm must be mature and mobile enough to be able to swim up the fallopian tubes and into the ovaries to fertilize the egg. In most cases of male infertility, any sperm that is present is either not high in volume or quality. Essentially, you wouldn't want my sperm forming a swim team because they wouldn't make it out of the starting blocks. Without ICSI, it would be much more difficult for my awkward, pimpled sperm who couldn't get off the wall to ask an egg to dance.

The second difference between the two procedures is where the eggs grow and develop. During IVF, the eggs are closely monitored by lab technicians while being incubated in the petri dish. The whole idea behind INVOcell, however, is to grow them in a device which is implanted inside the female to mimic a more natural environment. I never saw the device up close but the best way I can describe it is this: *Do you remember being a kid, going out for pizza, and begging for fifty cents to get the little toy in the plastic bubble with the colored cap on your way out? Well, INVOcell is like getting that thing shoved up your vagina. No, not the toy itself, but the little bubble container thing. I am not sure a mini-Cowboys helmet would fit too well anyway.*

They take this little plastic device or maybe it isn't plastic. *It can't be glass, can it?* Maybe it is plastic but a high-tech version for medical purposes. I don't know, but I am sure any medical professional or educated person on the subject is yelling out loud exactly what it is made of while adding the word "dumbass" after the explanation. Sorry, but I am not a doctor. I only watch them on TV.

Now that I have been completely sidetracked, let me get back to the story. They take all the eggs that have been retrieved, fused with sperm, and stick them in this device made of an unknown material. Just like with IVF, five days pass before clearer results are known regarding the development and survival of the embryos.

Chapter 26

Everything I shared with you, as informal or non-factual as it may appear, was all learned on our first visit. Well, let me say, I learned all of this on the first visit. Brandi had been researching by reading articles and being a part of fertility support pages for months by then. She had a notepad with more than twenty questions scribbled down that she would mark off as the doctor answered them, leaving the remainder for the Q&A session at the end. The doctor walked us through the process and showed us examples of various graded embryos, culminating with the perfect grade an embryo can achieve, a 4AA. Then again, maybe 5AA is the best grade an embryo can achieve. The world may never know.

The embryos had so many little bumps, bubbles, and definitions, but I couldn't see a huge difference between them on the chart demonstrating their growth levels. I just nodded my head in agreement with the assumed quality as the doctor went through his slideshow presentation, hoping he wouldn't pull out a pop quiz at the end to test my level of comprehension.

He then proceeded to tell us several stories about women in their forties and even fifties who were getting pregnant, not just with one baby but with twins. The chances of having twins with INVOcell/IVF is about the same as a natural pregnancy, but often the reason why so many more people have twins or even triplets with a medically induced pregnancy isn't due to random chance but instead on how many embryos people choose to implant. Any form of in vitro is expensive, takes time, and has a decent chance of failure, so some people are looking for ways to skirt the obstacles.

While it isn't proven to be true, and transferring more than one embryo only increases your chance of multiples, the thought of some is if two embryos are transferred at one time, then the chance of conception has just doubled, right? If both take, the chances are pretty good you will be having twins, but maybe neither take or one takes at first but doesn't end up surviving. In vitro usually requires a period of trial and error. If a person only has a few embryos to work with, do they want to blow their whole load on the first go? What if the timing wasn't right or another factor was preventing them from implanting? Those types of occurrences could make you run through your precious stockpile at an uncomfortable pace when you don't have all the necessary information for success.

Although we desperately wanted a baby, we were not overly keen on the idea of twins, so we didn't press him any further on the issue. Brandi did have a few questions, however, regarding success rates, medications, timing, etc. Most of those aspects were very dependent on age and egg supply and quality. Because of that the doctor stated our next step would be to get an AMH (anti-müllerian hormone) test done. Women are born with all the eggs they will ever have in life and each month an egg is released into the wild. Not all women have the same supply of eggs, however. As women get older and attempt IVF, they can be labeled with diminished ovarian reserve (DOR), meaning there aren't many quality eggs left to create a baby. The AMH test is designed to inform a woman how urgently she needs to act.

Usually, we were nervously waiting for *my* test results, but this would be the first time in a long time that Brandi was under the microscope. The doctor explained the test was very basic and results should come back quickly. There was no real reason to be alarmed due to Brandi's age and overall health. He ended up being right when her AMH results came back as a 3.4, which is a great number.

While that eased some anxiety, the thing I was most alarmed about was how much hellfire the whole INVOcell cycle was going to rain down on our checkbook. Having been caught off guard by medical bills in the past, I wanted to see the entire thing broken down with worst-case scenarios because worst-case scenarios are how I run my life.

The assistant walked us through the costs of the medication, the ultrasounds to monitor the uterine lining and follicle growth, the retrieval, the device, and the transfer itself. There was a section at the bottom with three different asterisked sentences indicating actions that could come up as the process progressed. The actions included (1) cryopreservation, which consisted of freezing any extra embryos beyond what would be initially transferred; (2) assisted hatching if the wall of the embryo needed to be punctured to assist with implantation; and (3) developing embryos in a petri dish if Brandi produced more eggs than would fit in the INVOcell device. With the way our fertility journey had gone up to that point, I knew there was close to a one hundred percent chance all three of the asterisks would be needed, so I calculated that into the total which came to roughly $13,000. That's a ton of money for something most people could accomplish in the backseat of a car for free.

Chapter 27

Television is a wonderful thing. I love it and watch quite a bit. I love sports, and together, Brandi and I enjoy watching shows on various streaming platforms. Whether it is a comedy or drama, we have all seen the script when a show is trying to develop or create a new storyline. An easy way to do that is to introduce a pregnancy. On some occasions, the pregnancy is planned and discussed by the couple but many other times it is introduced as an unexpected event that throws the lives of the characters into a frenzy. Either way, whether one partner looks at the other and says, "I want to have a baby" or they find out randomly, characters on television don't seem to have much trouble getting pregnant.

One evening we were watching *The Office*. Everyone was participating in a volleyball tournament at a company cookout. Pam hurt her ankle, and she and Jim decided to go to the hospital. Although we can't hear what is being said, we see the doctor speaking to Pam who begins to get a strange look on her face. It must not have been that strange because Brandi recognized it immediately.

Brandi's eyes were darting around the screen, putting the pieces together of what she was witnessing. "She's pregnant."

I looked over to make sure she hadn't leapt off the couch. "Hmmm…you're probably right."

Approaching a level that was quickly making this episode extremely unpleasant, she exclaimed, "That is such bullshit. What the hell? This is so dumb."

As I sat there listening to Brandi, since I could no longer hear the TV, I braced myself for a meltdown. During infertility, it was highly unknown which way an event was going to go. Would the event be contained within that small outburst? Would it result in tears and an hour-long conversation about why life wasn't fair to which I had no answers to offer, and positivity would be met with scorn because this was an emotional reaction, not logical? Since I couldn't respond that this was just a TV show and it didn't matter, I decided to join her side and came up with a soothing comment that would put this episode, *pun intended*, to rest. I didn't look at Brandi because eye contact could be devastating at that moment and said, "Yeah, stupid Pam."

Now I am not saying it was the first show or will be the last, but the first show I witnessed mentioning IVF, or acting like getting pregnant was more than a fluke, was *This Is Us*. Kate and Toby had gotten married and were starting to discuss having a child. Like many couples seeking infertility treatment, they tried the at-home method to find it wasn't producing the desired results. Although the couple did become pregnant naturally, they suffered a devastating miscarriage and were left to pick up the pieces of their lives. That event and the desire to have a child of their own led them to pursue IVF. Once Kate and Toby started seeking medical assistance, they were discouraged from even attempting IVF. Kate was severely overweight and older at the time, so the chances of a successful pregnancy were slim. The doctor initially refused to proceed with treatment due to the low rate of success.

Let's stop for a moment because this brings up a good point in the world of infertility. Fertility clinics pad their stats. Just like a quarterback getting a touchdown at garbage time, clinics are in the business of looking good. For someone who is seeking treatment for a high stakes medical procedure, statistics are usually sought out and deeply considered. When a person needs a heart surgeon and they have two seemingly equal choices except they find out one has a ninety-five percent success rate while the other has a seventy-five percent success rate, which option seems more appealing? Duh, the ninety-five percent doctor yo!

Statistics can be surface-level images that usually don't tell the entire story. Maybe the doctor with the seventy-five percent success rate really isn't that great and loses a lot of patients on the table. However, what if the seventy-five percent success rate is instead reflective of the fact that they accept almost anyone regardless of their condition or severity? If a doctor has a ninety-five percent success rate but only takes the easiest operations, are they really ninety-five percent successful or will failure hurt their chances of drawing in more patients for more money, so they turn away from the challenge?

Some fertility clinics follow that same formula. They want you to get all the tests and all the extras, not just because that is more money upfront, but because those precautions will increase their chances of implanting the perfect embryo at the perfect time. *What is wrong with wanting to implant the perfect embryo at the perfect time? Now you just sound spiteful.* Of course, nothing is wrong with that because that is the goal of every single fertility clinic in the world, but the issue comes down to the why. Are the clinics protecting you, your emotions, and your future economic state, or are they making sure they look good on the internet when someone Google searches "fertility clinics near me"? This all goes with the assumption that fertility clinics will even accept you as a patient in the first place. Your egg health, age, and a myriad of other factors contribute towards your eligibility for service at certain clinics. Any time a patient doesn't respond to a medication protocol, or an embryo doesn't implant, it goes against the bottom line, success, which feeds the much larger bolder bottom line, the all-powerful dollar.

I'm done vilifying fertility clinics because I am sure most are wonderful places, filled with great and caring staff who want exactly what you want. Let's get back to the show. Previously, on *This Is Us*, Kate and Toby were told the doctor would not proceed with IVF treatment due to their high risk of failure. Good news though because the doctor changed her mind and granted the couple permission to proceed. They go through the whole shebang and end up with one viable embryo whose picture they proudly displayed on the fridge.

If you have ever seen *This Is Us,* you know everything doesn't always end perfectly. For a moment, it was unknown whether Kate would become pregnant. In this case, Hollywood won out, and the transfer was successful. Many people are successful on the first transfer, but for every couple that is, there is one or even two that are not. I was glad that a television show went in a different direction by building a storyline around IVF and not just having Kate get knocked up after drinking a few martinis with a man she met at a bar that night. They certainly took the right approach, but Brandi and I have personally known couples who are perfectly healthy, in the prime of their lives, who didn't get pregnant on their first try or even their fifth. To present an instance where the chances of success were so despairingly low and have it work out perfectly the first time, was just another example of that candy-coated luster glossing over the ugly truth that is infertility.

Chapter 28

It was late March and time for our first step towards INVOcell. The first appointment had been a consultation but at this appointment, we would receive a calendar with important dates containing a medication protocol and when the retrieval and transfer would occur. We felt like it was the first time in a long time that we started moving forward again after being stuck on *my* broken track for so long. The funny thing about infertility is you can never get too comfortable in your current state because you never know what could come along and make you change course.

As I was driving to the appointment, I decided to call my urologist's office to see if they had the results of my final SA. "Yeah, I wanted to check on the results of my SA," I said in my "this is lame, and I want this to be over" teenager voice.

"So, the results show you had 300,000 per mL," the nurse stated in a deep but matter-of-fact tone.

"Um…I don't understand. What does that mean?" I was semi-frozen because I didn't know exactly what that meant, but I knew it didn't mean zero.

The nurse was looking at the results from that day in a vacuum because he failed to recognize the significance of this moment. "Well, it isn't a lot of sperm, but in about 3.5 mL you had 300,000 per unit."

Unable to process sperm fractions at that moment and wanting him to just come out and say a freaking final number, I asked, "Ok so how much does that mean I had?"

Attempting to keep me grounded in reality, he continued, "About a million, which isn't much though. That is very low."

"Ok, well, I had zero before so…I'll take it," was all I could muster as my head was spinning while I absorbed this news. My body was still driving my car, but my mind was over the moon.

Wow, one million sperm!? I felt great, like I could go parkour off the side of a building. I immediately called Brandi who was already in the fertility clinic's parking lot waiting for our appointment and shared the good news with her.

"Hey, guess what?" I asked, hoping she could sense my smile but that my joy wouldn't give it away.

Focused on the appointment at hand, Brandi wasn't looking to play my little games, "I don't know, what?"

"Well…I just spoke to the doctor's office, and…I have sperm!" I exclaimed into the phone.

I could instantly tell Brandi was stunned because of the lack of an immediate response. "Wait. What? No way! Oh my God, Jon. That is so awesome. So, what exactly did they say? Did you speak to the doctor? What are they recommending as next steps?"

After her barrage of questions, I suddenly felt unprepared, like I had dropped the ball. "Um, I don't know. He said I had 300,000 per mL in three and a half vials which equals roughly one million. I didn't ask anything else."

"You didn't ask any other questions?" Brandi's attitude contained a twinge of annoyance which faded quickly as she realized it didn't matter how many questions I had asked because I had sperm. "This is awesome. I can't believe it."

Thinking I had vanquished infertility and all its little demons, I asked, "Should we still go to our appointment?"

"Yes, *Jon*," she said, elongating the "o" as she often did after I said something ridiculous. "Having a million sperm won't get me pregnant. We still need to go to the appointment and let the doctor know. Let's see what adjustments we need to make."

I arrived at the clinic, and we informed the doctor of our very recent discovery. Because we had chosen a clinic that cared about us, there was no pressure to continue INVOcell treatments that day, and in fact, he even encouraged us to wait and see where this would lead. We went home, and I celebrated with a rewarding glass of bourbon, one that I had been saving for a special occasion but hadn't experienced since I bought it a year ago. At that moment, I recounted something I had failed to mention to Brandi. I had a feeling that the second surgery had worked because I swore I had been touched by the hand of God.

"I think God touched me a few weeks ago when I was driving to work," I remembered.

"Huh? What are you talking about? What do you *mean* God touched you?" Brandi said looking up from her book. When I could draw her eyes away from a book, I knew I had her interest.

"Well, I was driving to work one morning when I felt this strange sensation in my pants. It felt like a low rumbling vibration across my left upper leg/testicle area. I felt a whoosh like everything was released. It must have been God." (No response, just stares.) Realizing I was losing my audience, "Well, I don't know if it was or wasn't, but it could have been God. Either way, something shook loose because I have sperm now." Whether it was my leg twitching, the surgery kicking in, or the hand of God, whatever happened I hadn't felt it before and have never felt it since.

Chapter 29

Now, I know what you are thinking. A million sperm? Wow, what a big man you are! You finally did it! Well, slow your roll for a minute because like the nurse said, one million sperm isn't a lot. As you can see there are still quite a few pages left to read, so no, the journey didn't stop there. In the world of reproduction, a man needs at least five million or so sperm to try an IUI (Intrauterine Insemination), and even as high as forty million can still be considered a low sperm count. One million was a start, but it was nothing more than that.

We decided to see if we could continue to boost my count. After all, that was the whole reason we tried the surgery in the first place. If we could have children naturally and avoid the entire in vitro route that would be a dream scenario. With this revitalization, we went back to the urologist for what came next. It appeared the Clomid was working, but he wanted to add to it. Anastrozole and hCG were both prescribed to interact with the Clomid and make an Avenger-strength triad. They were prescribed in late March, but due to many reasons, the actual medication was not received until mid-to-late April. We hoped that delay wouldn't prove costly.

Anastrozole is a tiny pill that was easy to take, but hCG was a subcutaneous shot to the stomach which was something I had never experienced. I got a little bottle of powder and a little bottle of water, and after mixing, it needed to be refrigerated. But wait, there's more. In addition to the bottles, I also received sanitation wipes and a huge pack of those needles with the little orange caps that are very commonly seen on police shows for people who shoot up.

I didn't love the idea of taking shots twice a week. One of my last interactions with a needle was during a blood draw at the urologist's office to test my hormone levels. The nurse couldn't find my vein which about made me sick as she attempted multiple times. By the time she finished, I felt drunk. The kind of drunk where everything seems to be unsteady. I stumbled my way to the elevator, weak from blood loss, and up to the lab to complete my SA. I felt sweat pouring down my face and back as I slowly slumped over and started to slide down the wall as everything turned black. Realizing I had erred regarding the order in which my appointments should have occurred, I needed the first twenty minutes of my SA just to regain my composure.

The original plan had been for Brandi to administer the shots because I didn't think I could do it to myself. She had been feeling ill that week and when the moment came for the shot, her stomach and bowels started churning. She ran to the bathroom, got sick, and then proceeded to lay down on the bathroom tile and fall asleep. I needed to take them around the same time two days a week, and we were already off to a splendid start. I couldn't wait for her to wake up and pull herself up by the commode, so I did what any man would. I took a shot of medicine intended to aid women in getting pregnant, and I took it like a champ. Now that the first shot was out of the way, the next step was figuring out how I was going to keep it refrigerated on my trip to L.A. for work the following week.

The problem with transporting medication was that I had never done it before. I never took medication for anything outside of ibuprofen for a headache and maybe an occasional Tums. I knew enough to keep the original prescription bottles to help avoid questions, but I had no idea how to keep the bottle refrigerated and whether I could even bring needles onto a plane. I thought if nail clippers, more than three ounces of shampoo, or a half-eaten Snickers bar could have potential issues passing through security then needles surely must be a no-no.

I can hear it now. Well, why didn't you just put that stuff in your checked bag? Because I was cheap and didn't check a bag. My work wasn't paying for a checked bag, and I felt I could squeeze everything I needed into my perfectly sized carry-on. Packing needles for the first time was my only hang-up.

The needles I packed weren't giant cartoon sized versions but were needles a diabetic would need, thus making this whole episode seem blown out of proportion. The last thing I wanted, however, was to be stopped by security, called out in front of everyone for looking like a smuggler, and having to explain to my coworkers who knew nothing of my current situation exactly why I was taking so many drugs surrounded by ice packs to California. Talk about embarrassing.

I read beforehand that if someone needed to transport items such as medication or needles it is always a good idea to call it out to the person scanning your bags. That will lower suspicion and give them an idea of what they are looking for before they see it. After putting my laptop in a separate bin, my tablet in a separate bin, my shoes in a separate bin, my keys, wallet, phone, and belt in a separate bin, my backpack in a separate bin, and then forgetting about my wireless earbuds and putting them in a separate bin, I informed the person at the head of the conveyer belt in a low tone that I had needles in my bag with medication on ice to which he said, "That's fine," and proceeded to push my train of personal belongs down the line. I felt relieved and dumb at the same time. Thanks, TSA.

Chapter 30

There is a tragically funny aspect to infertility that I haven't touched much on, but I think now is a great time. The previous section took place in late-April, and now, with a flip of a page, we jumped to late June. Turning that page took a second, but what gets lost is that page took over two whole months of real-time to turn. Throughout infertility we found ourselves waiting…a lot. We would hurry from one appointment or event to the next to see if whatever we had been working on had yielded fruit, but in between each of those emotionally frantic moments, we'd wait.

When beginning fertility treatments, it can take months to even see a doctor for that initial appointment. Once you do meet and develop a plan, it is another month or two before that plan can be implemented. It took us a year from my initial diagnosis to have two surgeries and a zero sperm count. Talk about progress. It took another seven months to get to my second SA in a calendar year. It is essential to understand that this process doesn't happen overnight. The hurrying up and waiting takes a toll and keeps one from reaching true happiness. The lulls allowed us to relax for a minute because taking medicine wasn't particularly stressful, but it still took three months. Those three months were real and long and an ever-constant reminder of where we were, where we wanted to go, and where we couldn't be.

Since you now have a better understanding of time and space from an infertility galactic warrior, we can move on to the second SA of 2019. At that point, I owned that doctor's office when I walked through the doors. I looked people straight in the eye and spoke confidently right into their souls. I no longer had shame. Shame is something reserved for people with dignity. By that point, my dignity had been stripped away just like my underwear was about to be in a moment's time to complete my tenth SA. Was that actually my tenth time under the bright lights? I don't know, but it sure felt like it. If it was, I wish I would have asked for the punch card at the beginning that would have gotten me a free nudy magazine on my tenth visit. Either way, I had been numbed by the experience to the point I didn't care why I was there or who knew it. It was time to dive on in, and then hurry up and wait.

Chapter 31

The results came back, and *why don't you guess what they were? Now, don't be rude and guess zero or something like that. Why are you so mean?*

One million?

Five million?

Five hundred million?

    All very good guesses but the actual number was two and a half million. Woohoo!! Obviously, that is still a super low number but to go up two and a half times from the last count was huge. On top of that, the medicine took so long to be received, and I couldn't even take it for a whole three months. To us, that seemed an even better scenario because what would happen when I had another three full months to take the medicine? Would it double again or maybe even triple? If we could get to five million or so, we might be able to take a crack at an IUI and avoid full-blown IVF altogether.

    It seemed we had found a winning combination that would produce positive results. The plan was to continue what we were doing and try again in September. We were fully on board and started dreaming about having a family of our own, perhaps even naturally with no medication or assistance from science. We were encouraged to add a few vitamins and fish oils to continue to boost the count. If all I had to do was pop a few vitamins whenever we wanted to have a baby, then so be it. The three-month waiting period wouldn't be as bad this time because it was more exciting seeing something grow than be stagnant. People enjoy watching the rocket take off, not sit on the platform.

Chapter 32

Nothing really happened between the two and a half million SA and the one that was set for September. There was a lot of sitting around, not thinking about infertility, but at the same time not being able to completely forget. This wait was a little different though because we had something positive going. It was honestly the first time we felt like we had true momentum because "wins", as we called good news, were very difficult to come by. Sports have taught me that great teams string wins together, and these winning streaks are what put them in a position to contend. With the way we were stringing wins together, we were destined for the first-overall pick in the 2019 infertility draft.

We felt optimistically confident because of our upward trajectory, however, and I knew that if I said the same prayer and did the same things I did on that last SA, we would get another great result. It was hard to wait, but after two days I called for my results, holding out hope that we would be at five million or above and could start exploring an IUI. I reached the nurse who rustled some papers and then shared my new total. Drumroll.............................

"The results are in, and it looks like it's zero," the nurse said.

"Zero. What do you mean zero?" I asked as my stomach dropped.

He shuffled through his papers, and I could tell he was rereading the notes to be sure. "Well, I double checked, and yeah, it says zero," he said, seemingly unaware that he had just pulled the rug out from under me and smashed my dreams and visions.

Through the confusion and frustration, I managed to ask, "How can that be? I had two and a half million last time."

The nurse didn't know what to say next, so he used his programmed response. "Um, I am not sure. That will be something you'll need to talk to the doctor about at your next appointment."

I hung up, sat in my car, and stared off into the distance. Zero? Like…What? Huh? How? I was taking more medication than ever before and had been building the count. I felt like a racehorse that was champing at the bit in the starting gate, ready to take off, but instead of completing my mile lap and claiming glory, I simply leaned to one side and tipped over. That wasn't momentum. It was an implosion.

That moment brought me back to fifth grade basketball. We were especially bad that year, and the coach made sure to let us know just how bad. I was still at an age where every player received a participation trophy at the end of a season. We had just been mud stomped by our latest opponent when the coach approached the team huddle with a box of trophies. He could have easily handed them out and said thanks for playing, but he instead chose to inform us we didn't deserve trophies. How could we when we had been so bad? I remember him telling us that he didn't want to give us trophies but had to.

That was a powerful moment in an eleven-year-old's life, but the words found a strong parallel to my recent events. After over a year of trying, I had zero sperm. If my efforts were a box score, it would have been akin to one rebound, seven turnovers, and five fouls. Having sperm at one point offered very little consolation because I was back to square one. I was leaving the court of life with zero sperm and there would be no participation trophy waiting for me at the end of it. No one owed me anything. Instead of telling Brandi how I had come through for us, it was now up to me to have that familiar conversation that contained nothing but bad, sad news.

Chapter 33

When we first began our journey, we were in our late twenties which turned over into our thirties. We were in the heart of baby-making country, so naturally, we started seeing more and more people around us having children. We witnessed announcements on Facebook which included "our little pumpkin" or "our little turkey" is due whenever. I won't go as far as to gag, but if you have ever posted such a thing, could you have at least been more original with something like "our little gourd" or "our little green bean casserole"? Some of you have surely posted things like this and are now saying, *"Screw you. I'll post whatever I want, you cranky old man, and besides, those things are cute. What is your problem?"* So, if you have made that post, keep in mind that not only is it wholly unoriginal, but it is also highly annoying to people who are battling infertility.

If it was annoying to see a pregnancy announcement from someone we hardly knew, just imagine how crushing it was when those announcements hit closer to home. Take work for example. Brandi works in an industry that is predominantly female---education. She is a school psychologist and works in two different schools which doubled her chances of an encounter with a pregnant teacher. At one point there were so many pregnant teachers that it turned into a game that we weren't really playing but still somehow seemed to lose every time.

"Guess what?" Brandi would ask. She created an atmosphere that was so clear that I didn't have to guess, but I did anyway.

"Um, I don't know. What?" I said, instantly regretting my engagement.

"Another freaking teacher is pregnant at school."

These announcements had become so frequent that they no longer registered. I knew she was still deeply affected, so I tried to be sympathetic and get on her side. "Oh geez. That sucks."

Visibly frustrated and seemingly at the end of her rope, she exclaimed, "Yeah. That makes eight this year!"

Sometimes these news bulletins were met with unfazed numbness while other times it was a ticking time bomb ready to explode. Three, two, one, then tears. With every new pregnancy announcement, I tried to change the subject as quickly as possible or make it such a small deal that it wouldn't seem to matter. Each pregnancy came with a baby shower which produced more tears and prompted the mill of excuses to churn as to why she couldn't attend. Being in two schools made those excuses easier and more believable, but they still had to be produced and enacted.

The real kicker in those situations was when a woman was pregnant with her second, third, or even fourth child and the group insisted on throwing a baby shower. If the majority of the staff was male, a second or third baby shower, or maybe even the first for that matter, would have never crossed their minds, but schools are predominantly female. Oh man, if a woman was having a baby shower after her first child, and especially if Brandi was around long enough to remember she had already received one for a previous birth, game over. She would rant and rave and cuss using words no lady should know. Can you blame her though? It was mostly jealousy but justified jealousy. Those women had what she wanted and had seemingly gotten it so easily. Getting pregnant should be easy and for that reason, is a baby shower for the second or third time really justified? Some say yes, but someone going through infertility says, "Who gives a rat's ass?"

Chapter 34

The doctor called the next day to explain what may have led to the zero sperm count. Being a medical professional, he didn't explain it using these terms, but essentially, my testicles were like an old jalopy with a motor that didn't always crank. If you were made to read *The Grapes of Wrath* in high school, you might remember what a jalopy is and how to pronounce it. For anyone who doesn't know what that word means, I'll tell you. It means that my penis is like a piece-of-shit car. It's the kind you have to turn your key for fifteen seconds while it makes that choking sound because the engine won't turn over. Sometimes the car will turn on and get you down the road to have CVS screw up your prescription, and sometimes you can't make it out of the driveway. My manhood was a sputtering, occasionally working, jalopy. Good thing I wasn't already suffering from low self-esteem.

When my doctor gave me that "let's go out back and I'll make this quick and painless for you" Old Yeller look, I knew it was over. Stick a fork in me because I was done. We had spent close to $15,000 and about nineteen months to fix me, and I was no closer to fixed than when we started. It was truly sad when we stepped back and looked at it. That money could have been spent on European vacations, fine whiskeys, or Target shopping sprees. The world was our oyster.

Oh, and the *time*. All the wasted, never to be gotten back time. We could have started IVF months earlier: maybe not from the very beginning but at least before wasting over a year trying to boost my count. That one million sperm count had been a mirage in the desert but instead of it being a Dr. Pepper vending machine, it was a crate full of scorpions. Maybe it was more like a gaggle (*or is it a murder?*) of Sirens singing, "You have sperm. Spend more time making sperm," that lured us into false expectations until we crashed our boat on dream-crushing rocks. We might have reached our goal of natural pregnancy and avoided sinking into the whirlpool of infertility, but unfortunately, we weren't sailing in a swift and powerful battleship. No, we were stuck in a jalopy.

Chapter 35

Once we faced the grim reality that I was back to having no sperm and may never produce sperm again, the decision to proceed with INVOcell was instantaneous. The faint hope of raising my sperm count enough to attempt an IUI was all we were holding out for anyway, so the decision to proceed was easy. Our appointment was set for September and Brandi began taking birth control right away. To someone who hasn't been in the circuit long, taking birth control may seem like the completely wrong approach when trying to conceive. Birth control is supposed to prevent pregnancies, so why was it being prescribed before an IVF cycle? The purpose of taking birth control the month before a protocol and transfer date is to regulate a woman's system, assist with timing, and prevent cysts or any other irregularities from forming. The issue with Brandi taking birth control for just one month was that it created almost as many irregularities as it prevented.

The mood swings, tender breasts, raging hormones, and *oh the acne* that little pill produced. If Brandi wasn't complaining about how much her breasts hurt, she was running into the room asking, "Do you see this pimple? Look at how big this thing is. Was this here yesterday? They're everywhere!"

Brandi had taken birth control for many years, which looking back could have easily been forgone since her main squeeze was as sterile as a mule, but it was this rapid on, rapid off bit that concerned her. My main concern was if this was what birth control was doing to Brandi, then what would happen to her once she started taking the big drugs? The pills and shots we were paying thousands of dollars for certainly would pack a bigger punch than the free little pills she picked up from Walgreens. (Brandi doesn't go to CVS because she learned her lesson and isn't a glutton for punishment like me.)

We were told to call the office the day Brandi's period started and begin the medication regimen. Since we received our first consultation seven months ago, there had been some changes to the prescribed protocol. The company that sold our fertility clinic the INVOcell device had gone into the cable business. Well, not exactly the cable business, but you know how cable companies try to sell you television, internet, *and* home phone? Most people these days don't use a home phone and a growing number of the population has never had one in their home. That doesn't stop the cable company from creating a home phone bundle, however. Don't want a home phone? That's ok, but your bill will be more expensive. Why is that you ask? Why would I pay more for less product? "It's just our total home bundle sir." No good explanation. Simply just a "that's how it is" type of response.

That same "bundle" logic had permeated the INVOcell market because instead of the fertility clinic using their successfully proven medicinal protocol, the sellers were pushing the medicine they wanted patients to use. It's hard to not get sidetracked by the greed and immorality of big pharma, but let's save that for another time. The company's stance was that you could refuse to purchase their medicine with the device. That was your choice as an American, but guess what? Bam! Cable bundle. The price of the device went up so much that it ended up costing more than the device and medicine together leaving us with a forced no-brainer type situation. We had never done any version of IVF before, so how were we to know the difference? I surely wasn't going to pay a few extra thousand dollars to try the clinic's house-brand protocol, so we took the bundle hook, line, and sinker.

Chapter 36

Although we had been comparing prices, we couldn't buy any medication until Brandi started her period. While the pharmacies were fast about getting product ready and shipped, it did add an element of suspense as to whether everything would arrive on time. When there was a protocol in our hand that was parceled out day by day and one false step could be the difference between success and failure, wondering if we would have all the drugs in time was uncomfortable at best. For us, one of the best aspects of purchasing the drugs, however, was the amount of financial assistance we received.

Now, that last sentence is unfair because you can't hear my tone of voice nor can you see my eyes rolling to the back of my head, but surely by now you understand the last sentence is dripping with sarcasm. To be fair, we did receive a leaflet explaining how we could be eligible for up to seventy-five percent off our most expensive drug. The part that wasn't fair was that the assistance didn't consider anything but our latest tax information.

I believe that fertility treatment should be covered by insurance and be affordable to all people regardless of their income level. I imagine anyone willing to go through this horrid process has put some decent level of thought into having a baby and is serious about it. Some companies like Starbucks offer infertility coverage, which is where Brandi pressured me for months to become a part-time barista to get their infertility benefits. Insurance companies treat infertility like laser hair removal. It is seen as superfluous. Some may put those two cases on equal footing, but I tend to disagree. The neat thing is that once you are pregnant, insurance starts to kick in. They will hand you a bottle of water once you reach the top of the mountain, but they won't lend a hand when you are dangling by your fingertips on the edge.

Back to the seventy-five percent discount. It is great that any kind of discount is offered, but they take a very surface-level view of a couple's situation. Brandi and I aren't rich, but we are comfortable. We followed a strict budget each month and had been setting money aside for treatment for years. That method put us in a very good situation to be able to afford IVF, but once again, we are not rich.

When organizations only looked at our tax return and compared us to everyone seeking assistance, there was no way we would qualify. Plain and simple. While that sounds like entitlement whining, please consider our tax returns didn't take into consideration the tens of thousands of dollars we had already pumped into treatment and medical bills. We weren't starting IVF at square-one. We were starting way behind the eight-ball on this one. The discount request form didn't ask for that information though. There was no box to check informing them that $15,000 had already been spent up to this point. There was no additional paperclip icon to click and upload additional supporting documents showing the bills for appointments, surgeries, medication, etc. we had already endured. No, they looked at how much we made and wiped their hands of it. With little to no assistance from insurance or pharmaceutical companies, we were left to pick up the tab.

Chapter 37

Fertility medications are called "stims" which is short for stimulation and were intended to help Brandi create and grow follicles to a nice plump size. The more follicles that could be developed and grown to a specific size, the more that would release eggs that could be harvested, fertilized, and developed into embryos.

Let me stop here and say that I apologize for using the word "harvest" in the previous sentence and the ones to follow when referring to the stims process. I don't use it to objectify a woman's body to that of a farmer's field. Both concepts, however, focus on growing mass amounts and in most cases, using inorganic methods to produce the highest yield possible, so it isn't too far off, right? Maybe it is. I don't know. Well, if "harvest" is too cold of a word, please use the Find and Replace button in your head to substitute it for something softer like "gather" or "collect". Since you have accepted my apology, let's proceed.

Brandi's stims involved a long-Lupron protocol. Lupron's purpose is to suppress ovulation so that as the follicles develop and grow, they aren't released by the body as an egg normally would be during a woman's monthly cycle. One fear for some women, including Brandi, was they would go to their first appointment to monitor and measure the size of the follicles only to find that they had ovulated, and all that work and medication would be for naught.

To grow the eggs and make them nice and plump, a second medication was needed called Menopur. During a normal month, a woman's body produces one egg, and either that egg turns into a baby or is shed through menstruation. Menopur is designed to put a woman's egg making ability on steroids. Well, not really steroids. Well, I can't say that either because maybe it is…? Anyway, Menopur's goal is to produce a ton of eggs. More eggs equal more chances for a baby. Stims is a huge and vital part of any form of IVF. It lays the foundation for any other future attempts. I have heard about women going through a stim cycle and producing seventy or more eggs, but on the other side of that coin, some women take all that medication and end up with only one or two.

You may be saying, "Woah, seventy eggs! That sure sounds like success to me." Let me say that most people don't produce seventy eggs or anywhere close to that, and the more eggs produced is not always better. For some women, this overstimulation ends up putting them in the hospital with Ovarian Hyperstimulation Syndrome (OHSS). Going from one egg to even twenty at a time can be too much of a shock for the body and can be very damaging.

On top of that, stims comes down to quality. Just because a woman produces fifteen eggs doesn't mean she gets fifteen embryos. The eggs must be of good quality and continue to develop five to seven days after they are harvested ("Find and Replace"). If a neighbor brings over a bag of fifteen apples and right off the bat you notice that nine of them are rotten, then you only have six consumable apples. Over the next week you proceed to eat a few of them but then have to throw out the last three because they have turned squishy. How many apples did you get? *Sorry to throw out a second-grade word problem there but you get my drift.* At the end of the day, a higher number can certainly make a person feel more at ease, but even if only one or two embryos develop, as long as they are of good quality, there is still a chance for success.

Chapter 38

This is a good place to pause because I hear what you're thinking, "All this talk about growing follicles and your disgusting use of the word harvest is great information when describing how to make embryos, but I've been paying attention. It takes more than just an egg to make an embryo, so where the hell is your sperm during this whole process?" Well, if you had been patient I would have gotten there, but since you asked, I will catch you up to speed.

From the day it was collected at the biopsy, through the first successful breakthrough in the history of my sperm, my specimen had been kept at the same fertility clinic, FarEast. When they first collected the vials during the biopsy, we knew how much the initial charge would be, but we had failed to ask how much the subsequent charges would be for continued storage. It hit me, I think in July or August, that we hadn't received a bill for the second year of storage, and I was a little nervous because I didn't want potential bills hanging over my head. I figured it would be less than the $750 initial charge because that was for retrieval and storage, but boy was I wrong. The bill I received in the mail ran from May 2019 to May 2020 and was received in early October 2019, for $1,000.

I nearly dropped a load. A thousand dollars? For what? I understood that it took high-end technology to suspend my sperm in time and space and that we were bad consumers for not asking the question of future costs, but at the same time, why did the clinic not bring that up? I felt like a thousand a year to freeze sperm was a high price for the average American and might at least be listed in the brochure. The thing that got me was that the billing cycle started in May, and I received the bill in October. What the hell was I supposed to do with that information? I went to pick up my sword and venture back into the arena to fight the bloodthirsty lion that was trying to separate me from my hard-earned cash.

Chapter 39

I spoke to someone in billing at FarEast who explained that in May I'd had a choice whether to move the sample to Nevada and pay $500 a year to keep it in the desert or pay $1,000 to keep it at their local facility. *Bullshit.*

"This is the first I am hearing of this policy," I said, going from a four to a seven on the now-you're-making-me-angry scale.

The woman on the other end attempted to explain it away, by stating, "Well, we were purchased by a new parent company a year and a half ago and at that time we sent a packet containing paperwork in which patients were provided with that offer."

"I never received any such packet and was never provided a choice," I countered. Why would I need to keep my sperm close? It didn't provide me with comfort or love, so what difference did it make whether it lived on the north side of Indianapolis or in Nevada? "What is the charge if I transfer the sample out of your location? Would it be prorated?"

"Well, not really," she said, not giving an inch. "The billing cycle runs year to year so it would be for the full amount."

"I just received this bill a few days ago and in normal circumstances, I would have pulled my sample immediately upon seeing the price tag. The clinic I'm going to use only charges $350 for the year."

The back and forth continued until she broke. "I'll send you the paperwork and contract for you to sign. Once signed, I can work with you more fully, but I need that document signed first. What is your home address?" Something had changed in her demeanor as if she was suddenly playing from behind. The professional manner was still present, but it was clear she no longer held the upper hand.

Sensing this change in momentum, I pressed, "Can you send it electronically? I would like to see it tonight and resolve this immediately."

Usually, I signed most contracts on the dotted line without reading every word because ain't nobody got time for that, but since I had a high level of distrust, I started reading over the contract that night in depth. What started to become apparent was that FarEast wanted me to assume liability for something that should have been signed and processed way before the payment period began. Sure, they held my sperm, but I held the money. I felt confident enough that they couldn't just destroy it and knew I had leverage.

I consulted Brandi about whether I should sign the document. It was decided that this seemed a little too fishy and by signing I would be providing FarEast with a "Get out of Jail Free" card. That night, I emailed the clinic with a list of questions, referencing certain sections in the document that didn't seem right. Their response the following day was that a phone call would be best to sort these matters out. I tried to contact them over the next few days with little success. About four days later, I reached the first woman I'd spoken to, and I didn't even need to explain myself.

Sounding defeated yet apologetic, she began, "So yeah…We were purchased by a new parent company a while back, and it appears the paperwork was never mailed out to patients. If you can just get your sample out of our location ASAP, then there won't be any charge at all. It just can't take too long."

"So, how fast is fast enough? My initial cycle is in a few weeks. Is that enough time?" I asked, my voice swelling with pride over my impending victory.

"Yes. If you can get it out in the next few weeks, you will not be charged. If we hold it for another month or two, I can't make any guarantees."

Wow, what a relief! I had her repeat that several times and asked to notate my account because I wasn't going through that again. I was certainly glad to have avoided the charge, but are you freaking kidding me? If I had treated their contract like most others in my life, checked the box, and signed my name, I would have been on the hook. Are you freaking kidding me? The packet wasn't mailed, and they wanted me to sign a document six months later stating I would pay? I mean…are you freaking kidding me?

At this point, it may seem that I didn't want to pay for anything, and to be honest, that is true. I didn't want to pay for anything…ever, but I understand that is not how goods and services work. I one hundred percent believe that I owe what is due if it is fair and accurate. It is no secret that medical coding and billing can be riddled with errors, so it is reasonable to review and scrutinize charges especially when they do not seem to make sense. I am not saying with every bill I got on the phone and raised a fuss. There was enough coding that went well over my head that I couldn't have told you if it was right or wrong. The overall suggestion is if something looks out of place or doesn't sit right, investigate it. You might just save yourself a thousand bucks.

Chapter 40

The scramble was on to find a place that would transport my sperm while panicking that if I "took too long", they would slap that bill back in my face. I had no idea how long it would take or how much it costs to transport sperm. I reached out to my fertility clinic for advice on what type of company might provide that service because I thought that was smarter than searching "sperm carrier" on Craigslist. I shudder to think what type of person would have shown up for that.

To set the stage, let me point out that the mileage needed to transport my sperm from one location to the other was eleven miles. That's it. I wasn't asking someone to pick it up in Maine and bring it to Oregon. Nope, just eleven miles. They provided me with a company that was based in New Jersey. I didn't think that would be an issue because most companies can provide services outside their local areas. Well, not this one. The company in New Jersey told me the charge would be $750 for someone to drive a truck from freakin' New Jersey to transport my sperm eleven miles. At that point, I didn't know how much more I could take. An eleven-mile trip was going to cost $750? Ok, maybe that was the going rate for the service, but what got me was the fact that they would offer it to Indiana when it involved using a physical truck and driving over 1,400 miles roundtrip. Why not remain local and say we can't service your location? *I seriously can't make this shit up.*

After another day or two of searching for a business to transfer my sperm from the north side of Indianapolis to the slightly less northern side of Indianapolis, I came across a place called Fertility Couriers. The interaction with them might have been one of the best experiences during our entire fertility journey. I emailed the company stating what I needed and within thirty minutes I had a return email asking me to call for more information. Immediately the phone was answered, and the man explained how they sent a specialized tube that would keep the sperm at the optimal temperature while the two fertility clinics sent it from one to the other. Sarcastically to myself, I thought, "Wow, you mean you don't have to drive a truck cross-country to pick up my sperm? It's 2019 and shipping exists?" Although snarky, that was all there was to it. I am sure the tube itself was fairly advanced to keep everything from thawing and being worthless, but beyond that, it was too simple to believe.

What made it even better was that it was only going to cost $300 dollars. *Remember when I said I wipe my ass with hundred-dollar bills?* That was another example of when hundreds of dollars for an over-the-top task started to feel like a bargain. I figured that was the best offer I was going to get and since the guy I was working with had a pulse, I couldn't let that unicorn escape. He emailed me the entire time and kept me involved in the process from start to finish. I know this is starting to sound like a Yelp review, but positive experiences were so few and far between that I needed to highlight this one.

To keep things from being too easy, however, there was one more task to check off the list before the sperm could be transferred between locations. I had to have the document from FarEast notarized. I had just turned thirty-one at the time so at no point in my life had I been required to have a document notarized. I didn't even know how one would accomplish such a task. I asked around at work and was told that banks usually have a notary on staff. After work, I trekked over to my local Chase to sign the paperwork.

My bank account had been hacked a few months prior, so luckily, I had the wherewithal to know that I was going to need more than a teller to sign off. Before that, I had never spoken to one of the people that sat in the pen in the middle of the bank, so my experience came in handy. A short woman in her late thirties appeared, introducing herself as the notary, and led me around the small collection of cubicles to her desk. The whole time I was sitting there stone-faced but pleading in my mind for her to not look at the document too carefully. "Please just sign it. Don't read it. No questions. *Please.*"

"Can you explain the purpose of this document?" she asked, not bothering to look up as she rummaged through her drawer for her stamp set.

Damn it. Pausing to make sure I found the right words, I replied, "Um, yeah. It's to transfer my frozen sperm."

"Oh…ok," she said, looking down at the paperwork for the first time.

Other than "You're all set. Have a good day," those were the only further words exchanged, for which I felt truly blessed. I am the kind of person who doesn't like getting a haircut because it means I am held captive by a stranger who tortures me with the slow drips of small talk. Explaining to a stranger in the middle of an open bank floor that my ejaculate was being passed around from one location to the other left me red in the face. I shuffled out the door with my head hung low in case anyone else had heard my conversation, but as I exited the door into the cool fall air, I let out the breath I had been holding for the last six minutes. I knew that day's events meant I could never return to that particular Chase, but I felt so relieved to have that off my plate. I had my newly minted notarized document and was ready to get my sperm on the move.

Shortly after, the sperm arrived at my preferred fertility clinic, and I was so relieved to be done with that part. That was until I received a reminder bill for my $1,000 storage charge from FarEast. My first thought was, "Ah hellz nah. This can't be right." I got my contact on the phone and was hankering for a fight. With a tone silky as gravel, I started up with, "So, yeah...I just got another bill for $1,000 for sperm storage, but you told me all of this had been taken care of. What's going on?"

"Oh, of course, Mr. Spradley. You can ignore that bill. I will have it removed from your account," she said with the confidence a customer service representative has when they know everything is taken care of, and they only have to wait for the person on the other line to stop huffing and puffing so they can explain it to them.

I was pleasantly surprised when my request to notate my account paid off and thank goodness because this dog was about out of fight. They say, "All's well that ends well." I don't know if that is true, but I was just glad to see it end. I felt this moment marked the point in our journey where I could finally close the book on *The Case of Jon's Missing Sperm* and focus on the next daunting task.

Chapter 41

When Brandi started her stims protocol, one of the main concerns we had, or at least I had, was what this would do to her emotional state. I am bad with emotions. I have them, but I can't always control them. I don't always know what to do when others express them, and I certainly don't know what to do with my own. In college, Brandi and I would sometimes fight after a night of too much drinking, and I would try to douse her with ice-cold logic. Wrong choice. Cold, discerning logic is not what a boozed-up, hormone-enraged twenty-year-old woman wants to hear. I naturally thought she was being dramatic, and she thought I was being unreceptive. Both of us had at least one toe in the right.

Enough about those glory days though. It has been a long time since then, and we have learned how to avoid those fights by understanding each other and becoming better people. Undoubtedly, not abusing alcohol helps keep both of us in check too. My point is, we've had some issues with emotional understanding, and I was fearful we were heading back down that path. Pumping hormones and heavy-duty drugs into her system seemed like a potential recipe for disaster. Surprisingly, what hit the hardest wasn't the mood swings or high emotions, but instead, a flood of daily and unrelenting headaches that came crashing through.

Brandi has dealt with headaches for as long as I have known her, ranging from annoying, minor attacks to full-blown one to two-day assaults. Chiropractic couldn't eliminate the headaches, but they had been reduced. That was, at least, before the long-Lupron protocol. Notice the word *long* before Lupron as some women don't take Lupron at all, or at worst, as a small part of their regimen. At the same time, other women who suffer from endometriosis may have to take Lupron months before treatment to help suppress the hormones that cause tissue to grow. The word long in this case was defined by taking Lupron two to three weeks before stims and another two weeks into stims. To someone with endometriosis, this may seem like a cakewalk but for many other women, this is extended.

Usually, a migraine would be hit with an Advil and a Coke but taking that type of medication and adding caffeine was a no-no during stims. While Lupron wrecked Brandi's head, I soon found myself on a Gatorade/Powerade run to the grocery store. Electrolytes are supposed to be highly beneficial to physical recovery which makes sense because their commercials promote the product as body fuel, but in this case, we were simply looking for a way to keep her from going to bed by five-thirty at night because the pain was unbearable.

Pro tip: If you purchase one of these beverages to combat fertility medications, make sure you get the ones marked zero sugar. I wasn't told why. I was simply told not to mess that part up.

Brandi would spend the early evenings chugging whichever brand had been on sale that week, trying to stave off a migraine. It may have helped some, but it did not completely remove the pain during the long-

Lupron protocol. The only hope was that perhaps starting Menopur would bring about positive changes.

Chapter 42

Not only was the Lupron causing headaches, but I also failed to mention it marked the first time Brandi had to start taking shots. Sorry, I should have used the word *giving* there instead of *taking*. *Remember how I was nervous to take my first shot?* She was supposed to help, but instead of giving me the shot, she went into the bathroom, got sick, and fell asleep on the floor. I remember. It sounds bad to present it in that manner because it sounds like I was seeking revenge on Brandi when she was about to start treatment. *You're right that does sound bad, so instead of revenge, let's use the word payback...*

I wasn't really seeking revenge or payback but instead trying to encourage her to do the shots herself. I had done the first one by myself and was able to do the remainder that way. It simply put less stress on the whole situation in case, for some reason, I wasn't home or couldn't be home at the exact moment the shot needed to be done. Plus, it meant I didn't have to administer the shot. Giving myself a shot was one thing, but the thought of giving her one made me queasy.

When Brandi finally worked up the courage to give herself that first shot, she found it to be no big deal. "All done," she said beaming, holding up the syringe as if it were a sword that had been used to vanquish her enemies.

Seeing how I had taken shots for weeks; I was less impressed. I responded with, "See, I told you."

"Yeah, it really wasn't that bad. I was afraid after watching you take your shots," she wryly replied, seeing if I would engage.

"What does that mean?" I asked, picking up my proverbial syringe sword to do battle.

Unable to hold back her smile, she mocked, "Well, you always tensed up and flinched when you did them, so I thought they were going to be much worse than they actually were. You're weak." If that isn't the definition of marriage, I am not sure what is.

While the Lupron shots were winding down, the Menopur shots were picking up. Both shots were of the subcutaneous variety, and although on several occasions she would bark that "it burned like a bitch" and complained of some bruising, there wasn't much in the way of side effects while on Menopur which was a huge plus. We had an appointment coming up to measure the follicles to see if this protocol had done its job.

Chapter 43

We were met by the nurse who would be measuring our follicles and led to a room for an ultrasound. Brandi stripped down her bottom half and adorned the gown laying on the chair. I was nervous but excited to see how many follicles we had. A friend of ours had gone through this procedure a few months earlier and had come away with thirteen. Although the number of follicles doesn't provide an exact representation of how many eggs to expect, each follicle should have a decent chance of producing one, and to me, thirteen eggs sounded pretty good.

It was the silence that was most damning. If you have ever given bad news, you understand the awkwardness that can accompany it, and you want to make sure the bad news you are about to deliver is correct, so you pause. For a minute or two the nurse looked on the right side with a furrowed brow and the whole time I was yelling in my head, "Say something damn it. Say 'Oh, there they are. I couldn't see them at first because they were shy and hiding, but they have come out now. Oh, you have so many. So lucky.'" I didn't hear those words on the right side, and I didn't hear them on the left side. All I heard was, "I am only seeing two or three small follicles so let me go get the doctor to confirm what I am seeing is right." *Shiiiiiit.* Brandi's patented look-up-at-the-sky-and-fight-off-tears technique was in high gear at that moment and rightfully so. She knew this was bad. I knew this was bad. We both knew this was bad, and there wasn't anything I could do about it except hold her hand and pray.

I was raised in the Catholic Church by my mother who took me to Mass every Sunday. She wasn't content with just going to Mass every week though; no, it had to be the 8:00 a.m. service on Sunday mornings. I got two mornings a week to sleep in and one of them was donated to the Lord. After Mass, we had a tradition of getting gas, when on some occasions I would be lucky enough to get a scratch-off. We would then head to Target which was great because we had the place to ourselves. Even better, I was almost always rewarded with popcorn or a blue raspberry slushy.

As I grew older, the slushies started to dry up but the tradition of attending weekly Mass continued. I was enrolled in Catholic school from the age of six, served as an altar boy, and played in the Saturday evening music group which was the only way to drag my mother away from that dreaded Sunday morning service time. This base of faith has provided comfort and a place to turn when things become difficult in my life, and I leaned on it to get me through such moments.

My prayers were not answered in the way I had hoped when the doctor took over the controls and came to the same conclusion. The follicles were too small to proceed. We didn't have enough time to change the medications or make any adjustments. We could move forward with the whole shebang and hope that our tiny follicles would work, or we could cut our losses and lose the thousands we had spent on the medication. We took his advice and canceled the cycle.

The clinic was kind enough to not charge us for the ultrasound that day, and while we didn't expect that, it was much appreciated. A moment like that served as a positive indication we had picked a good, caring clinic. That act helped, but it didn't take away the sting of what had just happened. The money spent on the medication, the two months spent getting to that point, and the emotional capital spent was all a lot to take in and absorb. Brandi had spent almost two months wrecking her body and at the end of the day, we too were spent.

Chapter 44

Unhelpful Tip #2: Shutting down the conversation

Infertility is almost one hundred percent emotional, so as an outsider looking in, it can be difficult to engage in that arena. While you are busy following tip number one of not offering advice, try to also avoid shutting the conversation down because it is uncomfortable. Sometimes the topic is super-charged, borders on graphic, or is highly personal, but if the person experiencing infertility feels comfortable speaking to you about those things, it is your duty to engage. The last thing someone going through infertility wants to feel is that they are recounting their journey to someone who isn't listening or doesn't truly care.

Many people find sharing their journey with a few close family members or friends to be a therapeutic release. It is a lot to keep bottled up. At the same time, it is intimate, thus making it difficult to express. Most need an opportunity to vent, share emotions, or just be sad with the hopes of finding understanding. Everyone knows the frustration of trying to talk to someone who has their head buried in their phone scrolling Facebook. When someone is more interested in an acquaintance's post than the person in front of them, it can be quite upsetting to the person being ignored.

While that can be annoying, getting similar treatment when spilling your guts about your multi-year battle with infertility can be heartbreaking. Maybe that person isn't blatantly on their phone, but it is easy to tell when someone isn't fully listening. They may start washing the dishes, changing the channels on the TV, surfing the radio for a new song, or simply not providing their undivided attention. Others may be so uncomfortable about the subject matter or emotional content that they actively try to steer the conversation to something else, by using dismissive language to terminate the conversation.

While some may act purposefully, others may be more mindless, but the result is the same. The listener may see a canceled cycle or failed transfer as a "that's too bad" or "there will be a next time" but to the person experiencing it, it may have meant everything. Failure to seek understanding and provide compassion shuts the conversation down and puts the onus and weight back on shoulders that are already fragile.

Shutting a literal conversation down by failing to listen or engage is bad, but not attempting to create new dialogue can be equally destructive. Infertility is a tough one to check in on though because anything referred to as an emotional minefield doesn't sound easy to navigate. No one wants to upset people, and the fear of asking the wrong question at the wrong time makes people hesitate or avoid checking in at all.

The questions don't have to be deep, though. A simple, "How are things going?" or "Are you doing ok?" is perfect. Even statements such as "I have been thinking about you two and hope all is well," or "I know you had an appointment coming up and am praying for you," are excellent ways to touch base and let the person(s) seeking treatment guide the conversation from there. That is the beauty of those questions and phrases because they serve a twofold purpose.

1.   The person(s) seeking treatment knows you care and are there for them.

2.   It allows the person(s) seeking treatment to decide if they want to answer your question and if so, in how much detail.

Those questions are not so specific that the person(s) seeking treatment feels they have to provide details they would rather keep private or bring you up to speed on the latest setback. A simple "We are doing ok," or a "Not doing so hot," might be the result. Sometimes that is the best that can be done, but you will have made an effort. Other times, a word vomit might be coming your way, and you can then make plans to get together and discuss it in more detail if needed. Whatever the case, you continued the conversation and didn't leave them on an island.

Finally, beyond the questions, small gestures of kindness go a long way. During our journey we had friends write us personal notes, swing by with sunflowers just because, and even deliver a gift basket with items that put a smile on our faces. It doesn't have to be big, and it doesn't even have to be tangible. Sometimes continuing the conversation can be as basic as a hug, a supportive word, or being available to socialize and have a chill night. Acts such as these provide support and allow the person(s) seeking treatment to feel as though they can continue reaching out.

Going through infertility, we never wanted to feel like a burden. Not many people can handle a huge emotional dump because everyone has their own worries in life. It is easy to reach a point where the infertile don't speak about their journey because they believe others don't care anymore. Simple acts provide the reassurance that they have a support system that is willing to listen and offer assistance when possible. Even if the feelings and emotions of infertility are not expressed every day, knowing that others are out there to continue the conversation and truly understand, makes all the difference.

Chapter 45

The evening after our failed cycle, we came home and did what we had done so many times before when we had suffered a setback. Brandi cried while I tried to provide positive thoughts to help her realize it wasn't all bad. I tried to focus on the fact that although we had lost about $3,000 in medication, at least we didn't go as far as transferring and then failing at that stage.

"That has to count for something, right?" I would ask. She would agree but was still visibly hurt, so I would go into my next phase, apologetically wishful thinking. I would say things like, "I wish we didn't have to go through this. I wish all of this would go away, and we could just have a baby. I just don't know what to say. I just don't. I'm sorry." Sometimes I would just sit there and say nothing at all. Sometimes silence was simply the best way to ride out the storm.

While Brandi was deeply affected by these moments, she never became hysterical and could always bring it back together rather quickly. The problem was as soon as she would get it under control, I started to lose it. My anxiety would stir, and my head would do that whooshing thing. In and out. Back and forth. I would start to get an accelerated heartbeat and felt like I couldn't sit still. I had to do something but couldn't bring myself to do anything. When I got into moods like that, I tried to rationalize it and convince myself it would all be ok.

I would say out loud to Brandi but really to myself, "It's not that bad. This doesn't mean we can't have children or that it won't work. Maybe this wasn't the right protocol for you. Have other women had this type of issue? See, we aren't the only ones. You said this has happened to other women before, right? Didn't you tell me that before?"

Over and over, I played out all the scenarios. Surely this wasn't the end. This couldn't be the death knell. I kept a flurried but more positive mind towards the situation because I was much more ignorant. Brandi usually knew something I didn't know. In her research and support groups, she knew that some women simply don't respond to IVF medications. They are called "low responders" and essentially, they won't produce enough follicles to be successful. For a woman going through IVF, there are several ways a doctor can tinker with the variables through trial and error, but there simply aren't that many protocols to try. She feared that if the next protocol didn't work, it might be our last shot.

Chapter 46

Saying I was negatively affected by the pregnancy announcement of a friend sounds pretty sick and selfish, but it was true. The announcement of a true friend's pregnancy should have brought great joy and happiness, and while it ultimately did, the news initially struck me like a punch to the gut. There I was trying to keep it together and out of the blue, someone told me they were pregnant. For the most part, no one outside of our parents knew what we were dealing with, so I couldn't blame them for sharing. I actually wanted them to share the news with me because I really was happy for them, but it was that initial sick, jealous feeling that left me feeling dirty. I wanted to be all in with their joy, not straddling the fence between pleasure and pain.

I didn't like the way hearing a friend's pregnancy announcement made me feel. It became hard to shake as I kept thinking over and over how that should be us. There was no trying. There was no pain. Had they worked as hard as us to get pregnant? Hell no, of course they didn't. Most people don't have to, but it is akin to school or sports in which someone has more God-given ability to achieve goals without working as hard. The person who sweats and grinds starts to resent the person who naturally shows up unprepared and knocks it out of the park.

The jealousy and anger grew more intense as conversations began focusing on their pregnancy. We didn't care to ask many questions because it meant hearing answers we didn't know if we could handle. Other friends handled the questions, but even then, it was painful listening to the answers, knowing they hadn't done anything impressive to be where they were. It became unbearable as we sought to steer the conversation away from pregnancy and even sat a few events out, knowing the conversation would be squarely built around all things baby.

As we progressed through our journey, we encountered several couples who also faced adversity while trying to conceive. We would never wish infertility on someone out of jealousy or anger, and while these couples eventually passed us up and became pregnant, we found peace in their pregnancy. No one needs to experience infertility to completely love, adore, and cherish their child more than life itself. That unconditional love is unmatched and felt by so many mothers and fathers, but going through infertility at the very least, provides a leg up on the appreciation side. It's not to be taken for granted. Brandi and I can't look at each other when our future child is three and say, "Let's try for another one," and proceed to have sex. We fully understand how difficult it is to conceive and what is involved. The appreciation for the struggle and elusiveness is what we will hold close. No, we won't be able to love them any more than most parents love their children, but we will fully understand and appreciate the achievement of life.

Beyond the stomach-dropping moment that a friend's pregnancy produces, the ultimate knockout blow was delivered by a close family member. Brandi is the oldest of three grandchildren on her mother's side and like me, an only child. Because she was an only child, having the first grandchild was going to be a slam dunk, but her ultimate vision also included producing the first great-grandchild. That vision was shattered when her cousin, ten years her junior, got pregnant. Losing Brandi's dream produced a firestorm of emotion and profanity. We both knew this drastically changed her cousin's life, but it was still a tough pill to swallow. Brandi thought she at least had the benefit of time on her side when it came to her own family.

Watching people around us having babies was difficult. With every wedding we attended, we wondered when we would get to hear about their pregnancy announcement. The expectation was that *everyone* was going to be pregnant before us.

As time went by, we managed our jealousy better as we attempted to focus on only what we could control. We had no power over others, so why were we letting them affect us so much? Another couple having a baby had no impact on our ability to have one. It wasn't like there was a limited number of babies and everyone who got one before us worsened our chances. We decided to worry about ourselves by shutting the rest of the world out and concentrating on what was in front of us. We knew that our baby was still a distinct possibility, and no friend or stranger's pregnancy was going to alter that.

Chapter 47

Our doctor indicated that the long-Lupron protocol had likely over suppressed Brandi's follicle development, and he recommended we try the protocol they had originally laid out in March. It seemed like this wasn't the first time he had seen this from the "cable bundle" protocol. Not only did we lose money and emotional capital, but we also counted against our fertility clinic's success rate. A fertility clinic measures success based on pregnancy and live birth rates. If the protocol isn't good, an embryo transfer fails, or a woman doesn't make it to term, it affects their numbers. There is no way they wanted this baby more than we did, but they clearly had a vested interest.

The new-but-original protocol called for a whole new line-up. Letrozole and Gonal-F were substituted to increase follicle development, and Cetrotide was prescribed to stop ovulation. This time, medication designed to stop ovulation was going to be administered for three days, as opposed to roughly three weeks. We were hopeful but at the same time cautiously optimistic. A friend of ours had followed a very similar path and had gotten pregnant. We looked at this moment like rolling dice. Dice have no memory. Just because snake eyes came up nine times in a row at the infertility craps table, it didn't mean our odds would be any worse on the next toss. I was ready to roll again. "Daddy needs a brand-new baby!"

Chapter 48

Before Brandi could start any medications, we had to suffer through another long four weeks of birth control. *I know some of you are saying, "Damn, man. We already heard about all this. You take birth control to regulate, and then you get to transfer. What is the big deal about another few weeks? You waited longer than that between semen analysis appointments."* The big deal was that it was another four weeks. It was another four weeks on top of the mountain of time we had already waited to get to that point. It was another four weeks when we had been so close the time before. It was another four weeks and then we had to start the protocol. It was another four weeks when we were ready to be done with the whole damn thing.

Chapter 49

I think fertility treatment compares nicely to the game *Chutes and Ladders.* Imagine sitting down to play this game and the average wait time in between turns is three months. That would get old quickly, but you are still willing to play because the ultimate prize is worth it. You take your turn but realize that while you are moving square by square, others are landing on the ladders and immediately moving up them. You start to get a little frustrated at your lack of progress but keep hope that you too will land on a ladder space and start to move quickly through the board.

As you continue spinning ones and twos, moving space to space, you see that the friends you were playing with have already reached the top and completed the game. "How is that possible when I am back at space twenty? We all started at the same time. Actually, I even started before a few of them." You work to convince yourself that their turns and success have no bearing on your chance for success, so you continue moving forward. As you near the top, you pray you'll spin a three because your standard one or two spins will result in a chute that takes you all the way to the bottom, and the thought of starting over is incredibly daunting. The friends that had completed the game hung around to watch you play for a while, but they can only be interested in someone else's game for so long and leave you to play alone.

One! *Damn it.* You take the chute back down; not quite to the bottom but close enough to see the long climb in front of you. Panic starts to set in. How long will you have to play before the game is over? You start to realize that your turns are not unlimited and at some point, you will run out of opportunities. You try not to think about the spaces and pitfalls in front of you; all those chutes to slide down.

The worst part is you must be perfect. This isn't a game where you get close to the end, need seven spaces, spin a ten and stroll through the finish line. No, the spin must be perfect, right on the money. You don't get to be *close enough*. Games like these are sprinkled throughout childhood, like *Sorry!* where you are continuously knocked back from your current position, or *Candyland* where you get moving with a double red, high on life, and you're bouncing around like "*Oh heeeey* Gumdrop Fairy! Lookin' good" and then Bam! You find yourself at the bottom with that mud-looking-molasses-man-blob wondering what the hell happened. These are designed to be simple fun, but I never knew how much Milton Bradley and Hasbro were preparing me for a legendary ass-kicking.

Chapter 50

Other than pumping Brandi's body full of hormones and sending her into an occasional physical and emotional tailspin, the new protocol was off to a decent start. To help ensure it was going well, early monitoring was recommended. Normally, follicles aren't measured until a week into stims, but since we had royally failed the first time and had nothing to show for it, we scheduled an appointment four days into treatment. In case she wasn't progressing, we could make alterations to the medicine or the dosage to help promote better growth.

Have you ever been in an accident or had something semi-traumatic happen to you? If so, then you might understand that it can be difficult revisiting the scene. The sights, the smells, the way your hair stands up on the back of your neck can make those feelings rush back and make you flush with heat. When I was about eight years old, I attended a family reunion at Spring Mill. I wasn't at all interested in the reunion aspect, but I was extremely excited about the one thing that gets most kids geared up at that age; the lodge had a pool. I didn't get much access to one growing up, so staying at a hotel with a pool was a real treat.

The pool was interesting because it was both inside and outside, with a dividing wall I could swim under to reach either side. My mom doesn't swim, so she was lounging in the inside portion while my uncle was outside. My cousins and I were taking turns leaping off the edge of the pool, but as I was taking off, my feet slipped. I smashed my head on the side of the pool and sank to the bottom. My uncle was a strong dude and very capable of lifting an eight-year-old, but he required another man's help as I sank to the bottom.

I remember waking up inside the pool room with a crowd of people standing around me. My mom was holding a towel to the back of my head as my dad was being located to drive us to the emergency room. The lodge was in the middle of nowhere, so the drive to a hospital felt like forever. I should have stayed in the car because the pain that awaited was excruciating. The doctor stuck a needle in the gash in my head to numb the area before proceeding with six stitches. I have never forgotten that day because it is the closest I have ever come to dying. If my uncle wasn't there or hadn't received assistance in pulling me off the bottom, I very well could have drowned. I am not afraid of swimming pools, but I do tread lightly and can't quite shake the memories of that day.

The last time we measured the follicles was not a life-or-death experience, but it was a traumatic moment that we didn't want to relive. The fear was heightened for several reasons. First, we knew we could fail. This thought hadn't occurred to me the first time because I went through a lot of this journey at a high degree of obliviousness with a cruising altitude of steady ignorance. I never expected bad news because I didn't even know it was an option. Second, because of previous education provided to me by Brandi, I knew that if she didn't respond to this protocol, it could spell doom. There weren't limitless protocols we could choose from, so she might be labeled a "low responder". Not only would she be a "low responder", but she would also be an "unexpected low responder" meaning she had no excuse. There would be no clear explanation given the positive results from her lab work and AMH testing.

After we got situated, the nurse came in and started the exam. The doctor wasn't there that day, so she wasn't able to use a lifeline to ask him to come in for a second opinion if she couldn't find many follicles. Luckily, we were able to breathe when she found nine that measured in the acceptable ranges.

Exhale. This is an excellent example of the constant events throughout infertility where we would spend the week with our stomachs in a knot. I swear to you that the week before an appointment I would get bloated, have stomach aches, headaches, and every ache in between. My stomach would just churn and churn, and I would make constant trips to the bathroom. Maybe it was my IBS, but I think it was from a different acronym, IVF. If we received good news, I would feel instantly better. I never used to fully appreciate the phrase "I feel like a weight has been lifted from my shoulders," but now I get it. I don't know if that weight was on my shoulders or my abdomen and gut, but either way, it certainly felt like it had been lifted, if just for a moment.

Chapter 51

Brandi showed me a video about Jimmy Fallon and his wife discussing infertility and the lengths they went to conceive. They joked about infertility and when presented with certain treatment options they would say, "We certainly won't do that," only to find themselves doing that exact thing out of desperation a few months later. Fallon even kept magnets in his pants, and while I don't fully understand that one, it goes to show the things people are willing to do.

After the revelation that Jimmy Fallon and his wife struggled with infertility, Brandi found other celebrities who used some form of in vitro to get pregnant. It was refreshing to know that others fought the very same demon, but it was also interesting that the Fallons, like most others, didn't discuss their struggles until after they had children. Why hadn't they discussed these trials as they were occurring?

I ask this question, but at the same time, I cannot blame them because at first, we didn't discuss our infertility with others either. We told people on a need-to-know basis like certain family members and friends who would notice if Brandi wasn't drinking at a bar. We told the people we couldn't hide from, not everyone we came across. Why don't more people discuss infertility, though? *It happens to one in eight couples, so surely someone you know is experiencing it, right?*

Maybe it's because it seems so easy for others to get pregnant that talking about infertility almost feels taboo. It is a very personal and emotional subject that couples go through, so perhaps it simply can't be broached with everyone. Another aspect is the feeling that it might not need to be brought up at all. With every new test or treatment there is a feeling of, "Maybe this is it. Maybe it will work, and we will be pregnant. Once we are pregnant, bells will chime, and all will be right with the world. We can make our announcement on Facebook and watch all the likes and comments rack up." I know that was true for me. The thought was if we get past this point, it will probably work. Then who else needs to know? They will find out with the rest of the world. That concept was mostly an illusion, however, almost as if infertility were a fish swimming in a stream. We would see the fish and go to grab it, but the water reflected a different position than where the fish was, and we would end up with nothing but wet hands.

This fear of failure can also keep people's mouths shut during treatment. Making our situation more public would have garnered more questions and recounting of failures. I will watch the same highlights and classic games of my favorite teams' victories so much that Brandi, who doesn't follow sports, knows what is going to happen. I have seen the moment hundreds of times when Tom Brady is intercepted by the Colts which sends them to the Super Bowl. But if a clip comes on showing Peyton Manning being intercepted in the 2009 Super Bowl, my heart sinks. That interception happened over a decade ago, and I can't watch it. If I can't do that, why would I want to recount over and over how a transfer failed and we still aren't pregnant?

Internalizing and keeping things to oneself can be a great coping mechanism. Some need support groups, but others rely on their partner or themselves for stability. Infertility hurts, and not living that hurt every time someone asks how treatments are going is a positive. Throughout the process, we wanted to be able to provide positive updates, but those updates were slow forming, if they existed at all.

Being insulated by secrecy had its pros, but feeling like we weren't the only ones out there was even better. When people speak up and bring others into their fertility journey it can produce positive results for other couples who are also affected. Inspiration, hope, resources, information, and support are all provided when people are aware that infertility is real and isn't occurring only in their lives. Silence has never created a dialogue or moved the needle. The infertile can become connected and not feel they are on an island with no way off. Being alone is not a feeling most human beings are comfortable with because we are social beings. If people going through infertility feel that no one is out there, they may give up more easily and surrender the dream. Sometimes it only takes one connection point to truly make the difference.

Chapter 52

Over the next two weeks, Brandi continued to have blood draws to better understand her hormone, estrogen, and progesterone levels and make sure everything was where it needed to be. There was a follow-up appointment to measure the follicles, and to our delight, they found two more that were approaching a viable size. We were finally nearing our first fall harvest, albeit in early January, and had the chance to fertilize up to eleven eggs.

There was one more step between us and retrieval day. The trigger shot. The trigger shot is an intramuscular shot that needs to be injected thirty-six hours before retrieval. The shot fills a woman's body with hCG, the same lady drug I took to create sperm. Essentially, it's designed to stimulate the ovaries so the mature eggs can be released. It was incredibly important that this shot was taken at the proper time: if too late or too soon, we could have some serious issues achieving success.

There was a fundamental difference between the trigger shot and the ones Brandi had been taking up to that point. *I gave you a hint. Did you catch it?* "Intramuscular" was the biggest difference -- meaning it had to be injected directly into the muscle, not subcutaneously. The more substantial difference was that I would be the one administering the shot, not Brandi. I was initially confused as to why she wasn't capable of giving herself an intramuscular shot in the ass, so I took it upon myself to play the hero. I had never given a shot to another soul in my life. I was terrified. I had been through the wringer over the last few years, but surgeries, blood, and needles still gave me the willies. My friend had to give his wife a trigger shot, and he couldn't do it. She had to go to the hospital and have a nurse do it while he nearly passed out just from watching.

I was going to have to be tough no matter how easy it was supposed to be. There are lots of YouTube videos out there of people administering these shots, none of which I could bring myself to fully watch due to the gruesome nature. Some of the tips I picked up were to pretend it was a dart and kind of flick it with your wrist. I am no good at darts and end up hitting the wall more than the board, so that didn't help. Another pro-tip was to practice on an orange as that closely mirrors a human's flesh. I don't care to eat oranges very often, so I failed to buy one of those too. With all tips wasted, the nurse drew a circle on Brandi's lower backside and told us that was the spot to aim.

If Brandi was nervous, then I was *tweaking* as I picked up the needle and prepared to plunge it into her. Just like darts. Just like darts, I kept saying over and over in my head while practicing a flick of the wrist motion. Oh, that's much too slow. That would hurt her. Well, that is way too fast. That might kill her. With ten repetitions under my belt, I was ready to step up to the plate. Just like I was taught in Little League, I got into my stance with my feet shoulder-width apart, kept my back straight, and stared down my target.

It was almost in slow motion. I had the rhythm measured perfectly. The angle was forty-five degrees, and I nailed the fifty-point center of the bullseye. It couldn't have gone any better.

"Jon! What the hell?" Brandi yelped, clearly unimpressed with my abilities. "You need to count. Why did you not count out loud? You need to count next time because I was not ready for that. That hurt like a bitch."

"I'm sorry. This is really painful for me to do," I whined, trying to retreat to the other room.

Brandi's eyes immediately narrowed with an are-you-kidding-me look, as she retorted, "Painful? You're not the one getting their ass punctured."

Like a batter who hits a fly ball to the fence only to be robbed of glory by the center fielder, I too did not find the success I thought I might. Although I didn't hit a home run, I still did what I needed to do. Perhaps I did well enough for it to be considered a sac fly.

Chapter 53

I know you all won't believe this when I tell you, but guess what? We added another layer of complexity on our transfer day. Yes, I know it's hard to believe that we might experience another potential pitfall in the middle of the pothole we called life. Recall that I have a jalopy for a penis. It starts and then stops and then sometimes doesn't start at all. Well, because of this, my urologist informed us that if my thawed sperm was not of adequate quality, more may need to be extracted through another surgery. He was nice enough to offer the surgery for free, which made us think he felt bad about the first surgery not working and took pity on us. We would only be responsible for anesthesia and potential hospital fees. Delightful! The prospect of another surgery to get fresh sperm because the three vials they had sucked from my body might not be good enough was a cherry on top of my medical saga.

Relief came when we walked in the door, as the doctor greeted us saying there was sperm in the vial. A fresh sample would always be preferred, however, and they would continue to monitor it while I attempted my own extraction. Their masturbation station was a bit different as there was no leather couch, but instead, there was a conference room style chair with two thin little arms which made for a very awkward setup.

Once I had completed my business, I rang a doorbell to let them know I was done. I found the experience akin to when you ring the doorbell at someone's house. Sometimes you aren't sure you pressed it hard enough because you don't hear the chime. You have two choices at that point. You can either ring it again and look like the jackass who gave someone three seconds to come to the door or you can wait and see if anyone comes to the door. Being the nervous person I am, I decided to wait. After about a minute, I realized no one was coming, so I pressed it harder than before and heard the doorbell chime. Knowing I hadn't passed the simple test of ringing a doorbell, I felt less confident in my ability to produce a worthy sample for conception.

The embryologist came to the door to collect my sample. At the urologist's office, I put my sample in a quasi-medicine cabinet, waved at someone behind a desk to let them know I was done, and then walked away. This time was different. She came into the room and looked through my paperwork and asked me a few questions. I sat there holding my cup with my hand wrapped around it, pressed up against my body, trying to keep it from view. I felt so ashamed. What made it worse was the embryologist wasn't some sixty-five-year-old lady but a small, cute woman, about my age. For some reason that made it worse. Why couldn't she have been hideous?

I must have been hiding my sample extremely well because after a few moments she looked around the room and then at me. "Where is your sample? Do you have it?" she asked, still unsure of my sample's location.

"I have it right here," I said sheepishly, as I started to hand it to her.

Looking as if this sort of mix up happens often, she calmly directed, "Oh, you can hold on to it. I'll show you where it goes."

There is nothing worse than trying to hand a young woman a cup of your semen, and she rejects it. Such embarrassment. To top it all off, when I got to the lab, like an idiot, I tried to hand it to her again.

"Just go ahead and put it in here," she said, pointing to the microwave-sized incubator.

"Ok," was all I could muster as I proceeded to melt into the floor. I shuffled out of the room with my eyes pointed down to locate Brandi who was awaiting her fate.

Chapter 54

Once I was safely in the procedure room, Brandi and I patiently waited for what came next. Although this wasn't going to be some major surgery, it did require an anesthesiologist who came to our room to give the basic rundown of what she needed to do and what could be expected afterward. Brandi was already very nervous and anxious about the procedure at hand, so the semi-graphic description of an IV needle going into her arm and having medicine course through her veins was almost too much.

She finished explaining her job, and all Brandi wanted to do was lie down because it had made her sick. What was making me sick was the thought of everything that could go wrong. Our doctor came into the room and helped put one fear to rest by telling us that my fresh sample had sperm in it. The old jalopy came through in the clutch! It wasn't much, but since I only needed one sperm per egg, eleven would be the maximum required. He proceeded to tell us how good of news that was because the sperm they thawed from my first vial was ok but not great, and he had been considering whether to thaw a second vial or not. What a crushing moment that would have been if we had to burn through two of the three vials, of what could have been the only sperm I possessed on this Earth, on the first transfer. That was a worry for another day, however, because there was enough sperm left over from my fresh sample to be frozen for a second round of IVF if needed. We hoped it never came to that, but it certainly provided peace of mind.

Chapter 55

It was time for Brandi to be wheeled back to the operation room. We were told it would be a short procedure that would last roughly fifteen minutes. After she left the room, I began my count. When a deadline is approaching or you want a day to last forever, time seems to fly, but when you are in the middle of a gut-wrenching experience, the clock appears to be broken, crawling towards its destination. I thought maybe I should go on the internet to pass the time. I would then mentally slap myself out of it and think, you can't scroll through ESPN right now. Your wife is experiencing what could be a life-altering moment and you are going to read an article about the NFL playoffs? Get a grip man and focus on the task at hand. So, instead of mindlessly scrolling my phone, I waited.

I waited, checked the clock, waited, checked the clock twice more, prayed, checked the clock again, waited, and checked the clock five more times after that. I started to get worried around minute seventeen. This was supposed to be a fifteen-minute procedure, not sixteen and certainly not seventeen. What was going on in there I wondered? I knew it was bad, and I kept yelling in my head, just be done. Just roll her back in here and say, "Surprise! We found twenty eggs and they all look perfect. Congrats, dad."

At that moment, they brought Brandi back into the room. She was awake but was in what was described as a "twilight" state, meaning she was in hazy town---not quite there but not quite out of it.

The doctor came into the room with his normal kind demeanor that offered no clues as to whether we'd hit the jackpot, stating, "We got eight good looking eggs."

"Oh, that is so good. Isn't that good Jon?" Brandi replied in a half-asleep tone.

"Yes, that is great," I said, hesitantly excited. I was confused, but I didn't want to express my thoughts out loud for fear of upsetting Brandi. My head started running the numbers and recalled we came in with eleven follicles. What happened to the other three? Come to find out, the two that were found on the most recent ultrasound didn't develop to the proper size and another one was on the gimpy end. Brandi informed me later that one of our friends had thirteen follicles but only retrieved seven eggs. We had actually done quite well.

I didn't linger on the fact that three of the eggs didn't make it because eight was still an incredibly strong number. The next step was to see how many were mature and to fertilize them. That part was going to take a few hours, so we were encouraged to get some breakfast while we waited. We found a Bob Evans not too far away and guess what we had on our minds for breakfast?

Chapter 56

During breakfast, we discussed an interesting concept that a friend going through treatment mentioned. It had never really dawned on us, but all of our future children were potentially being conceived on the same day. Think about that for a moment. Every child we might have was created on the same day. *Now, don't be a jackass and say that same logic applies to someone who only has one child or twins.* The point is it doesn't apply to someone who might have up to eight children, octa-mom notwithstanding. Would we have some semi-daring and seemingly funny story about conceiving our children in a porta-potty at a rock concert? No, but I'll take my epic journey of testicular surgeries, sperm growing, egg harvesting, and sadness and stack it up against anyone who wants to tell a "cute" story about how they screwed in a broom closet. Bitch, please.

It was a very philosophical breakfast because the conversation eventually turned to prior discussions regarding extra embryos. Originally, I thought three children sounded like the perfect number. Brandi was never quite on board with three because we would be outnumbered, and because of that, I was swayed towards having two children. Infertility struck and the idea behind having even one child grew exponentially distant. Once we started seeking treatment, however, we began to understand that we might have embryos left over after we had created our perfect family. If we happened to have a few embryos left over, what would we do?

One of the reasons we chose INVOcell instead of traditional IVF was for this very reason. INVOcell involves less medication and therefore, less stimulation. Less stimulation leads to fewer eggs/embryos which leads to fewer ethical decisions. The thought of potentially having fifteen embryos through IVF would be great in the sense that we could have fifteen chances at a child. Hopefully, it wouldn't take fifteen attempts to have two children, though. What to do with all those extra embryos was a very daunting thought that would certainly challenge our morals, ethics, and overall practicality.

If we found ourselves in that scenario, we would essentially have three choices: dispose of the embryos, use them by attempting compassionate/less medicated transfers, or put them up for adoption. Disposing of them wasn't an option for us. My mother used to make me roll a tube of toothpaste so tightly, pushing everything up towards the end, just to make sure it was completely empty. The thought of disposing of embryos was not a path we wanted to explore. The moral was: if I had to use all the toothpaste in the tube, how could I possibly not use all of my embryos?

A compassionate transfer was another option. Beyond never having any children, my next biggest fear was that this whole thing would go in the opposite direction, and we would end up with more children than we wanted. I was fearful that we would go through this process, end up with the perfect number of children or come to accept the fact we would never have children, and then somehow, at forty plus years of age, we would have a child which would throw a wrench into what we thought would be the rest of our lives as a childless couple.

Continued transfers also made us slightly nervous because what if they took? We wouldn't be able to afford eight children, but thankfully, it would most likely never come to that. If we completed more transfers, we could allow the embryo a chance at life but in a much more natural way with basically no medication. After participating in something so unnatural for so long, the thought of going au naturel sounded pretty good.

The last option was embryo adoption. It sounds almost as weird to talk about adopting embryos as it does picturing it. I imagine an orphanage full of little bubbly looking blobs sitting around, hoping their future parent(s) is on their way. Some couples don't make it as far as we did and need to adopt an embryo from another couple to start their family. If we chose that path, we would have to participate in an extensive selection process to choose who our biological children would be raised by. We would be holding the fate of another family in our hands, which was not an overly ideal place to find ourselves because the pressure to get it right would be immense.

On the surface, it seemed uncomfortable knowing our flesh and blood would be somewhere in the world, and we would most likely never meet them. To wake up in the middle of the night and know a part of you is out there would be quite surreal. The question of how we would choose and would we be comfortable with our decision was very heavy. On the one hand, it was a strange feeling that would take time to make peace with. On the other hand, we would be helping provide life to a child, while also helping a couple who was in desperate need to hold and love that very same child. Who were we to deprive someone of something like that? We knew how much blood, sweat, and tears it had taken to get to this moment, so how could we turn a couple away who was just as longing? It was probably one of the most thought-provoking breakfasts we had ever had.

Chapter 57

Upon returning to the clinic, we received some good news. All eight of our eggs were mature, had undergone successful ICSI, and were waiting in the INVOcell device to be implanted. That was reassuring to hear because not all eggs retrieved are usually mature and some do not survive past the point of retrieval. At the time, our doctor was assisting another patient, so his partner would place the device. The substitute was a grizzled veteran in the infertility ranks and had done too many cycles to count. He was focused on achieving results, not always patient comfort and care. I wasn't allowed into the procedure room with Brandi, so I waited until she got back to be filled in.

When she returned, I could tell she couldn't wait to tell me something due to her eyes being large as saucers. "Oh my God, Jon," Brandi softly whimpered.

"What?" I asked, anticipating details of what had occurred.

As if she was still wrapping her head around what had just happened, she continued, "He was so deep. Like he shoved his entire fist up there."

Seeing this as an exaggeration, "No, he didn't. Come on."

"Yes, he did. I swear he was at least wrist deep and he kept shoving and poking trying to get that thing in there. I had no idea he was gonna go that far in there. It hurt so bad. On top of that, he kept making a bunch of old man jokes that weren't funny, but I tried to laugh anyway. Do you know how hard it is to fake laugh when someone is up there like that?"

I'm sure the trauma her body experienced from having eggs extracted a mere three hours ago helped amplify the pain, but neither of us thought that was how the device was placed. I thought it would be like a delicate operation, the kind you see in space movies when the astronauts are faced with certain death unless they can guide a small capsule through something the size of a pinpoint. Instead, Brandi was treated like a human Muppet whose handler was having a bad day. Neither a warning nor a gentle approach was offered. The good news was that it was over, and she and her bow-legged-self had a nice long car ride home to recover.

Chapter 58

During traditional IVF, embryos are kept in a lab while an embryologist monitors their development, but in INVOcell, Brandi acted as the human equivalent of a petri dish. The "at home" portion of development took five days, and it was a unique experience for sure. Some women reported being able to feel the device inside of them while others hardly noticed at all. Brandi didn't necessarily feel the device, but she sure knew it was in there.

Brandi is a school psychologist who works mainly with preschoolers. Even the infertile understand how active a three-year-old can be as it involves a lot of catcher-like squatting positions to get onto their level. Because of that, the fear of the device squirting out was real. She had to modify her scheduled activities and ask some of her peers to take over her responsibilities because high levels of activity and motion were discouraged while the device was in place. It got worse though. Work-related activities were altered to fit her current situation, but some things in life just couldn't be avoided -- like going to the bathroom.

Brandi was afraid to go to the bathroom because she had read about cases in which the device fell out of some women. What percentage of women experienced this? No idea, but it didn't matter. It happened to one woman so it could happen to her. That was the thing about being on the infertility train for so long. Once we realized there was a chance for something to go wrong, we figured we'd be the ones to run off the rails. It was truly sad, but the worst-case scenario started to become our most expected outcome. Brandi started to think, why wouldn't I be one of the 0.02 percent of women who have the device fall out of them when they pee? Everything else has gone wrong up to this point. Let's just add another "You're a freak" statistic onto the pile. The jaded feeling grew so strong that it was hard to count on success for even the most basic tasks.

Since the act of taking a poo takes certain muscles, some of which put stress on the vaginal canal and the device, Brandi thought it would be prudent to pinch her vagina together to keep the device from slipping through. Had she received this instruction from her doctor? No. Was it something that should be done? No. Was it going to make a damn bit of difference? I doubt it. The paranoia had kicked in and if pinching her vagina closed was going to make her feel more comfortable, then who was I to take away her peace of mind by pointing out how irrational it was?

Chapter 59

After five days of successfully not grunting the device out of her body, we were ready to receive a report of how everything developed. Thankfully, the process of removing the device was much less traumatic than the insertion. Brandi was prescribed Valium, so perhaps that had something to do with the ease of extraction. Perhaps it was because some man wasn't trying to force something up there that wasn't meant to be inside a person. Either way, it was a much more pleasant experience.

Our doctor revealed we had five great looking embryos. At that point, the little ball of cells is called a "blastocyst", but since I get confused about the different terms and stages, I will stick with "embryo". Anyway, if you have been keeping score at home you would know that we went into the appointment with eight eggs and now the doctor was telling us we had five left. What the hell happened to the other three? Come to find out, the three didn't advance in their development enough to be viable. Of the three, one didn't fully fertilize or survive long after being placed in the device. The other two ended up not progressing enough to be considered for implantation.

Whether that was a good rate of success or not, the news was wholly disappointing as we had seen our chances of success almost cut in half. The good news was the five remaining embryos looked strong and healthy. It would still take a few more days before we were totally out of the woods, but the embryologist would continue to watch their development and inform us of any changes.

One was set to be transferred that day and the remaining four would be frozen. The process of implanting an embryo ended up being one of the easiest things we had done while trying to conceive. We were both taken to the procedure room where Brandi was propped up on a table in stirrups. The doctor was very pleased with the embryo quality and was even more excited that the one we were transferring was already hatching. Hatching is just what it sounds like. Think of a baby chick bursting out of its egg. The fact that our cute little embryo was already hatching meant that it was ready to attach to the uterus and implant.

That embryo was a real go-getter. It was ready to rumble, and all the doctor had to do was get it there. The embryologist handed the doctor a tiny plastic wand that contained the embryo at the very tip for implantation into Brandi's uterus. That was it. Like an Olympic relay team handing a baton from one runner to the next, the process went off without a hitch. On the way home, there was one stop to make. Brandi had read in her support groups that McDonald's fries helped with implantation. There was something about the salt that made everything stick. I highly doubted the validity of that belief. Regardless, I didn't fight the logic because if it meant I got greasy food on top of what was turning out to be a pretty good day then I was all for it.

Chapter 60

Two days later, I got a call from Brandi. Since the year was 2020, the only reason a person would even think about calling another person was that they were either old, or they had bad news. Since Brandi was younger than me, I knew it could only be bad news. The instant I picked up the phone her tone said it all. Normally I would be greeted with a "Hey what's going on?" or a "Real quick...", but this call started with a "Hey, do you have a minute?" that was said with a mix of annoyance, frustration, and sadness.

"The embryologist called and left a message saying they were able to freeze two embryos, but the other two didn't make it. On top of that, the woman at the front desk said I owed $2,000 for the last appointment. I told her I had already paid the $1,400 and to check her records but the other $600 was to freeze your fresh sample from the transfer. I just can't right now. Can you call them back and get more information?" she said in a frustrated tone.

Absorbing this news like so much debilitating news before, I responded appropriately but not strongly enough to make the situation worse, "Hmmm. Well, that's disappointing. Did they say why the other two didn't make it?"

"No. She left a message but didn't say. Please just call them back because I can't," Brandi said. It was if the phone was on fire in her hand, and she couldn't stay on the line a moment longer.

Knowing there were certain aspects of this journey that were mine to handle, I didn't press further. "Ok. I will try to reach them."

I reached out to the clinic and spoke to the embryologist who explained that two of the embryos didn't develop properly and had collapsed in on themselves. In the end, they were not strong enough to survive. The good news was we had two perfect embryos that could be frozen. Not much of a consolation prize when our chances were, yet again, cut in half. I was beginning to have an eerie feeling that I had seen this movie before.

It felt a lot like *Willy Wonka and the Chocolate Factory*. Five children find golden tickets and get a private tour of the factory. One by one, the children keep getting picked off and eulogized in song by Oompa Loompas. I felt like that was what was happening to our children. We'd had eleven follicles, and suddenly, three drowned in the chocolate river, three turned into blueberries, and the final two were deemed to be rotten and dropped down the garbage shoot. I was hoping against hope that Charlie was implanted deep within Brandi's womb and wasn't going to be disqualified because he decided to steal fizzy lifting drink.

On top of that bad news, the other issue that stuck in my craw was the fact we were being charged $600 to freeze a few thousand sperm. I was very happy to have produced those sperm and to keep them for a round in the future if needed. I wasn't pleased about this surprise bill, however. The total cost for keeping sperm frozen at their location for a year was $350 but the cost of freezing just one vial was nearly twice that?

The embryologist explained that it didn't really matter the amount of sperm, or to a point, even the number of vials that were to be frozen because it took an entire kit each time. I don't know what goes into a kit, but I sure as hell know how much it costs. God forbid I ever needed to tap into that vial, but if I did, it would be like uncorking an extremely expensive bottle of champagne.

Chapter 61

George Michael once sang the words, "I gotta have faith," and while I can't imagine it was a song about the trials and tribulations of infertility, there couldn't be many truer words to describe the process. You absolutely must have faith when embarking on a journey like this because it's seemingly never-ending and fraught with pitfalls. One must learn to trust their doctors and believe they truly know what's best.

Brandi and I joked from time to time that everyone going through infertility should be provided with a coach; someone who has been through the process or at least a person well-versed in the language of infertility that could take couples by the hand. For some people, claiming to be self-taught is a badge of honor; something they can brag about. Whether it is the musician who was never taught to read music but can play a perfect concerto or a craftsman who picked up tools at a tender age and mastered a skill through tinkering and experimentation, it's great that people can be self-taught. Does it mean it is always the best approach? Most of us are not virtuosos and need coaching and assistance. How many errors and pieces of scrap were produced by the craftsman's experiments? Sometimes you can "go it" alone, but it isn't the easiest or most efficient path.

Without a dedicated person to see us through, the task of navigating infertility fell to two completely green individuals with little to no idea of what to expect or where to turn. That is where faith came into play. We had to trust the process that was being laid out before us. We had to have faith that the doctors knew the best course of action and were prescribing plans that were tailored to our unique situation, not a cookie-cutter blueprint.

We went into these appointments unsure about exactly what needed to occur, but we didn't go in stupid. Faith doesn't need to be blind. While it is not always the best coach due to its differing opinions and information, Google provided many helpful and informative resources to help us understand what questions to ask. We also consulted other resources such support pages, books, and other forms of literature to make sure we were smart consumers. If you go to buy a new phone but have done zero research, the chance that you leave with something you don't totally love due to ignorance or the salesperson pushing their agenda is quite high. The same rule applies to infertility. Do your homework and understand what to ask. A doctor is never going to want to be told what to do, but a *good* doctor should be willing to listen to your input and ideas and be flexible with treatment when able.

Chapter 62

We were down to three chances to have a baby and one of those chances was already in progress. We received a blurry photo of our transferred embryo that looked very similar to a low-quality image of a shooting star. Since "low-quality image of a shooting star" was too long and not cute enough of a name for our ball of cells, we decided to name the little one Bean.

Bean subsisted on a steady diet of progesterone that was administered through Brandi's backside every day at precisely 5:30 p.m. When a woman is naturally pregnant the body supplies all the progesterone a baby needs, but when you are trying to have a baby through a series of chemistry experiments, this has to be supplied through a syringe at the same time every day through the first twelve weeks of pregnancy. The shots started a week or so before the transfer, and they started cramping my style immediately. That sounds selfish because I was only giving the shots but having to be at home every day at 5:30 p.m. wasn't always easy.

It wasn't just that we had to be home at a certain time for the shot. There was also a routine that followed which took up even more time and started to interfere with other events in our lives. Progesterone can hurt. It can hurt going into the body, and once in, it can start to form knots. Some suggestions to combat this were to ice the injection area beforehand, but others would say that icing makes the progesterone congeal which leads to even bigger knots.

We took the suggestion of rubbing the area out to help disperse the medicine. To accomplish this task, I would stand behind Brandi and smooth out the spot with a rolling pin. It sounds weird, but after all, that is pretty much the purpose of a rolling pin; instead of dough, we substituted human skin. After that, we applied heat. Brandi would sit on a heating pad for thirty minutes to help dissipate the medicine even further. The heating pad became so much of a constant that we were able to determine which side we needed to alternate to on a given day based on the latest position assumed by the heating pad in the chair.

By the middle of the second week, our method was starting to clash with the train wreck we called life. I wanted to attend an autograph signing downtown at the mall, but until the night before, I had completely forgotten it started at 7:00 p.m. It took us about thirty minutes to get downtown, and we still had to eat and get in line early. I had an "Oh, shit!" moment when it dawned on me that the timing wasn't going to allow us to attend the event.

"We can't go to that autograph thing tomorrow," I whiningly said, realizing this whole process was continuing to strip me of bits of joy.

Brandi was caught completely off guard as my outburst broke the peaceful silence that had occupied the room just seconds earlier. "Huh? Why not?" Brandi asked, annoyed at my aggressive approach.

My agitation rose because she clearly wasn't understanding the complete thought in my brain that had only been verbally expressed as a random fragment. I shot back, "Because we have to be home to do your shot and that leaves us no time to get downtown."

"Ooooh, I see. Well, can't we just do it in the car?" she easily concluded, owing her enlightenment to the fact that her judgment wasn't clouded by anger.

Hmmm. Now there was an idea. I wasn't crazy about it, but I *really* wanted that autograph. Normally when we'd go downtown, we parked on the street. This time, however, we felt privacy would be best since our activity might look shady. In hindsight, it probably looked even shadier shooting up in a parking garage though. We went to the lowest level and tried to park away from other cars because with our orange-capped needle it looked like we were injecting something more sinister than baby food. I looked over both shoulders to make sure no one was coming and jabbed it into Brandi's exposed butt. Thank God a cop wasn't driving by because I am sure we both would have been detained. It went off without a hitch, but there was still one hurdle to overcome. Brandi couldn't use the heating pad while we ate stale Chinese food in the mall food court, so she did what any self-respecting thirty-year-old woman would do; she stuffed two hand warmers down her underwear, pulled up her yoga pants, and prayed they stayed in place.

If you thought that was the only example I could provide of when nightly injections affected our lives, you'd be wrong. We were on our way to Friendsgiving, which is a very Millennial thing to do by the way, and found ourselves on the road once again at 5:30 p.m. While the timing wasn't ideal, we certainly weren't caught off guard. At about ten after, we started looking for a place to stop so we would have plenty of time to get everything ready. We found a Cracker Barrel for restroom purposes but weren't dumb enough to try anything there. I have never seen a Cracker Barrel not stuffed to the gills with cars. It can be 7:00 a.m., 11:00 p.m., or even Christmas day, and it seems like everyone within a thirty-mile radius has chosen Cracker Barrel for that day's meal.

We eschewed the notion of having a parade of people walk past our car and drove across the street to a rather empty At Home parking lot. Just like in the parking garage, we handled our business in the car. We were on Brandi's right butt cheek that night, but since the angle was difficult to maneuver with a twenty-inch rolling pin, we decided it would be best for her to just get out of the car. I didn't get out of the car and roll her out. No, that would look too weird. Instead, she simply walked around the parking lot, rolling a baking apparatus on her ass. Cars would drive by, and I could tell they were looking in our direction wondering what the hell was going on, but there wasn't much we could do.

When I was younger, my family went shopping at an outdoor mall, and as the day dragged on, my dad grew weary and decided to take a nap on a bench. I don't mean he sat down on a bench and let his head nod for a few seconds, I mean he stretched out longwise on the bench and went to sleep. He later said he was too old to care what people thought of him, and he was going to do what he wanted. We had also reached the "completely horizontal nap on a public bench" portion of our lives, where this whole thing was getting too old, and we didn't care what people thought of us. If anyone wanted to gawk at Brandi rubbing her ass with a rolling pin in the middle of a parking lot, then that was their problem, not ours.

Chapter 63

During the two weeks after the transfer, Brandi started having some slight pregnancy symptoms, but it was difficult to know exactly what they meant. Like I said earlier, a woman who gets pregnant naturally starts producing progesterone which can lead to pregnancy symptoms such as tender breasts, tiredness, nausea, etc., but during IVF it is impossible to distinguish between actual pregnancy and the side effects of the medicine. I asked almost every single day how she was feeling, partly because I wanted to make sure she was ok, but mainly because it was the only way I could track progress.

Because it wasn't my body, I was unable to gauge exactly how unusual a symptom might be and how strongly it might be felt. Every time Brandi would mention a symptom I would hop on Google and search for something like, "tender breasts during pregnancy". This would allow me to better understand whether what she was feeling was good or not and whether the timing seemed to match up with when she should be experiencing it. Brandi would tell me not to read too much into the symptoms because it could just be the progesterone mocking pregnancy, but it didn't matter because I couldn't stop analyzing everything.

My investigative mind soon became my biggest detriment when Brandi started bleeding. She bled on day six post-transfer. When she told me, my heart sank and my mind raced. In a low and fearful voice, Brandi approached me saying, "I had some spotting today."

"Um…ok, that doesn't sound good. Was it a lot?" I questioned, trying to stay cool on the outside while suppressing the sheer terror on the inside.

She attempted to keep me from panicking, while at the same time feeling the need to inform me of the level of concern she felt. "No, not a lot, but it's still not good."

"Didn't you say one of your friends had bleeding during her early pregnancy?"

I could see the wheels turning and a moment of acknowledgment that things might not be as bad as they appeared. "Yeah, that's true. You're right. She was farther along, but you're right. It may be ok."

While I usually didn't associate bleeding and pregnancy as a good thing, I thought maybe it wasn't all bad. Since I was now gripped with fear but hoping everything was ok, I immediately looked up "bleeding during pregnancy" and got hundreds of results. Many women shared how they had experienced bleeding during pregnancy with some describing "implantation bleeding" which is light spotting that can occur in about a quarter of pregnancies when the embryo implants into the uterine lining. As the embryo nestles in, it can cause some light shedding of the lining which may seem alarming but could be a good sign. I read and read trying to convince myself that spotting was actually a good thing, and by the time I had finished my research, I truly thought implantation bleeding could be what Brandi was experiencing.

My doubts started to grow, however, when the bleeding continued. Implantation bleeding should only last around one to three days and start to trail off. Not only did the bleeding remain consistent; it persisted for six days. Once I realized the bleeding carried over into the fourth day, I started to get nervous. I kept a brave face and tried to be positive, but Brandi was starting to fade. We were scheduled to have our beta test, which is an early pregnancy test that measures a woman's hCG levels, two weeks after the transfer. We were discouraged from taking an at-home pregnancy test sooner because it could produce a false negative, but we couldn't wait. Two days before the test, Brandi took an early detection pregnancy test but couldn't look at the results.

"You aren't even going to look at it with me?" I incredulously asked.

"No. I know it didn't work," she said, moving into the living room to sit in the farthest possible place away from the pregnancy test as if it contained some sort of radioactive property. If she created physical distance, she could create mental distance from the inevitable pain.

Her reaction was understandable but irritating. "How do you know that? You don't know that."

"Yes, I do. I haven't felt anything for a few days, and I just know it didn't work." Although she was walking away, I could picture the tears welling up in her eyes, cascading down her freckled cheeks.

I went down to my knees and stared at the test resting on the kitchen counter. "Well, I am going to watch and find out."

A minute passed as I tried using Jedi mind tricks to materialize a faint pink line on a completely blank space. I stayed like that for three minutes, out of fear that if I turned around, I would match a visual to the sound of tears I was hearing behind me. That would make it real. That would make our first shot at a baby a failure, and I was tired of failure.

Once I reached the same conclusion that her prescient mind had revealed days earlier, I knelt by her side and held her hand while she cried.

Growing up, my family would make the five-hour drive to Illinois to visit my grandma. I loved visiting my grandma. She had a local candy store where I was allowed to scoop as much candy as I wanted from glass containers into a brown paper sack, and I got to watch Nickelodeon on cable television. We didn't have cable, so watching *Rugrats* was a real treat. The best part about visiting my grandma was playing cards. She was in her mid-seventies when I was about six so the one card game we could play together was War.

We would flip the cards down onto the footstool situated between us with her seated in her chair and me on the floor. Slap! She would throw out a king, but I would toss an ace onto the footstool just as fast. When I instantly saw I had won, I would gather the cards quickly and add them to my pile.

"You cheated," she would say with a smile on her face and a grandmotherly twinkle in her eye.

Feeling under attack, I would protest. "Nuh-uh. I beat you, but you didn't see it. Look here," I would say, showing her my cards.

Turning to my mom on the couch she always jested with, "He cheats. He won't even let me see the cards!"

I knew I hadn't cheated. She wasn't as fast as me. Looking back, joking or not, I realize how she perceived the situation. Here she was throwing out a king, feeling good about her situation, only to be bested by an ace, seemingly time and time again. I too felt we had thrown out a king at infertility. We had a perfect embryo, implanted by science at the right time, and life trumped us with an ace. Things were flying around us so fast that we couldn't even see the cards before they were swept off the footstool in front of us. All we could do was feel cheated.

Cheated as I was, my body produced no tears that night because my logical brain had told me this would most likely happen. It is a tough task: trying to trick one's brain into believing something it knows to be false. I wanted to believe. I even tried to believe, but at the end of it all, I just couldn't get on board with the notion that the bleeding was no big deal. Did Brandi's bleeding have anything to do with the lack of a positive test? I don't know for sure, but I do know it couldn't have helped. All I knew was it was the biggest blow yet, and my fear was it may not be the biggest blow yet to come.

Chapter 64

Two days later, out of formality and a desire to obtain concrete proof, Brandi had her beta test. Any remnant of hope vanished when the news came back as we expected. Shortly after finding out Franklin Roosevelt died, Harry Truman, after being sworn in unexpectedly, found himself speaking extemporaneously with the press. He told them, "…I don't know whether you fellows ever had a load of hay fall on you, but when they told me yesterday what had happened, it felt like the moon, stars, and all the planets had fallen on me." Infertility is a lot like that because everything can be humming along when you get whacked. It is a lot like a cartoon character who is walking down the sidewalk and a piano falls out of the window above and crushes them. The only difference is that the cartoon character is magically better in the next scene while the sting of infertility takes longer to recover from.

Mental and emotional recovery can be a double-edged sword. On one hand, no one wants to be upset and let sadness linger for weeks or months after a heartbreaking event, but on the other hand, how much of a positive was it that after less than two days we were able to discuss our next steps? Outside of the night we found out I had no sperm, this was the worst moment we had shared as husband and wife, and we were ready after less than forty-eight hours to look ahead. Were we becoming hardened by the process? Since we knew we were attempting something with a fifty percent success rate it allowed us to visualize a realistic outcome of how this might not work the way we wanted it to, but to answer the question, yes, I think we were hardened by the process.

I have never fought in a war and therefore cannot make a perfect comparison, but I have read books and watched movies about it. It seems in most cases a group of green recruits spends time bonding in boot camp before being shipped off to battle, and upon arrival, they look around and see the grizzled veterans standing before them making snide comments about how the newbies don't know what's about to hit them. While the sights, sounds, and smells of battle quickly overwhelm the new recruits, the veterans are hardly fazed. They have been in it so long and seen and done the most unimaginable things that it no longer produces much of a shock.

I read a book about the Vietnam War in which soldiers had been assigned the job of transferring the dead into body bags. The author was writing from a firsthand account about picking up limbs of other humans and placing them in bags to be flown back to the States. Of course, there were instances when it caused him discomfort and even sickness from doing a job like that, but it was part of his job. It had to be done, and because he had been doing it so long, he didn't fall to pieces every time. Even the most horrific tasks can become commonplace and lose their effect.

In no way am I putting the horrors of war on equal footing with infertility, but I am trying to illustrate that infertility is the enemy and treatment is the battle. We found ourselves doing things we never thought we would have to do or thought we could do, but here we were, moving forward. That soldier had a job to do, and we felt we did too. In a job, you don't get a choice of whether you want to or not, you just do it. We had seen and experienced too much to let this failed transfer bring us to our knees. Time to get back to work.

Chapter 65

Unhelpful Tip #3: Miracles

We have all heard a similar story about a horrible wreck in which the car is completely smashed with smoke billowing from the engine, and the driver walks away without a scratch. You can hear someone proclaim, "It was a miracle no one was hurt." Miracles do occur in life, but they don't occur every day. That is the reason they are called miracles in the first place. If a miracle were an everyday occurrence, it would just be the way things are. Miracles are mentioned commonly and almost used as old wives' tales when discussing infertility. Although the desired intent is to provide hope and reinforce the concept of never giving up because you don't know what could happen, the effect on an infertile person is usually negative.

Recounting miracles to a couple going through infertility is neither helpful nor inspiring. People love telling the one where a couple has tried to have children for years, tried every type of procedure, and then decide to adopt, only to find out they are now pregnant naturally. Oh, glory be!

Brandi loved to say adamantly, "Well, that is great for them, but that will never happen for us."

"Yeah, probably not," I would respond, hoping to avoid the wrath from being directed at me, "but maybe."

"You don't have any sperm, *Jon*. That's not possible. We aren't just going to one day wake up and find out we are pregnant. Those people who experienced that were most likely cases of unexplained infertility."

It sounded harsh, but it was true. It was true I didn't have sperm, or at least not enough to ever conceive naturally. Wasn't going to happen. It sounded harsh because it dashed that hope. Knowing something isn't in the cards can be a hard pill to swallow, and all that "uplifting miraculous story" did was remind us to not count on it. It wasn't going to do us any good.

Another miraculous story that did no good was about a woman seeking IVF treatment for her second child. After her first child, the doctor said it was a miracle that she even had her first because of diminished ovarian reserve. Her AMH was a 0.25, which is terrible, and she was given a one percent chance to give birth to a second child. Her body didn't have many eggs left, so things had to start moving quickly. She attempted a round of IVF and produced one egg. Just one egg and it wasn't of very good quality. The IVF cycle ended up being unsuccessful. With her chances falling at a dramatic rate, a natural, unmedicated IUI was attempted, and glory be, yet another miracle. Even this woman who was running out of eggs and was told she had a one percent chance succeeded. If that wasn't the miracle we needed to draw strength from, then what was?

I believe in miracles as much as I believe in winning the lottery. They happen but are rare. This type of holding out hope creates a blind sense of reality. I am sure those stories are true, but it wasn't our lives. Those stories serve the same function as telling someone you are having a rotten day, and they say, "Well, my cat died yesterday if that makes you feel any better." How the hell does that make anyone feel better? How does someone else's miraculous success do anything for me other than get me pissed at why I can't be that lucky? If something is based on statistics and numbers, then that information carries more weight. A fifty percent chance of success across the board tells me a lot more about my situation than that one time a woman had a one percent chance to have her second child and it worked. Excuse me for passing on the "glory be" because I ain't convinced.

Chapter 66

A fresh, perfect looking 4AA embryo was transferred but didn't take. That summed up where we were and what we knew. Brandi spoke to me before our first follow up visit about the possibility of doing an ERA cycle (endometrial receptivity analysis). Most women's bodies are set up for transfer on day five, however, this isn't always the case. An ERA takes a small sample of the endometrial lining to determine what the optimal timing might be for women who have had a failed transfer for no apparent reason. The results could provide some valuable information, but this was one of the first times we had to have a conversation about how to proceed.

I kid you not when I say that almost every other decision we made required almost no discussion about which route to take. Of course, we would talk about it, but there was never a debate. If the doctor told us to go one way, we did. If we saw a choice that needed to be made, we made it in instant agreement. We weren't necessarily being mindless sheep but saw the path as the correct one to be on, so we continued straight ahead.

The ERA test was different, though, because we found ourselves at a crossroads. My logic was based on *playing* the odds, which were in our favor. The test might not reveal anything. In that case, precious money and time would be flushed down the drain. Brandi's logic was based on *improving* our odds. If the test proved that our timing was incorrect, then our chances of having a successful transfer would increase substantially by making the necessary adjustments. My ignorance, which seems to be a common theme at this point, took Brandi time to overcome. Although I wasn't all-out fighting her on the idea, I wasn't convinced at first because I didn't want to necessarily be convinced. Being convinced meant going with the ERA. Going with the ERA meant waiting, and I was *so* tired of waiting.

Waiting, waiting, waiting. With dashes of heartache and soul-crushing news sprinkled throughout, waiting comprises the backbone of infertility. That's pretty much it. Just waiting followed by some heartache, followed by waiting, more heartache, waiting, a piece of crushing news, and more waiting on top of that. Rinse and repeat. I didn't want to wait.

To obtain the data we needed, a mock transfer would be required. Brandi would take birth control for one month and then Estradiol pills the second, just as if she were gearing up for a frozen transfer. One difference would be instead of transferring, the doctor would scrape out a portion of her uterine lining for testing. *Sorry for the word "scrape". That was Brandi's word of choice, so I thought I would pass it along.*

The other difference can be found in the first, "instead of transferring". We would spend an entire two months just going through the motions. I went on a trip to Iceland when I was about twenty-three years old to visit a friend. I had an amazing time seeing glaciers, smelling sulfur gas everywhere we went, and camping out in the middle of nowhere under the stars. The trip itself was memorable, but the trip back was something I would like to forget. Being twenty-three, I purchased the cheapest possible ticket which required a ten-hour layover in Boston and a thirty-hour total trek to get back home. By the time the plane landed with bags in hand, I was more than ready to get home and collapse into bed. The problem was I had to wait on the shuttle to take me back to my car, and it took forever. I was so tired, so cranky, so pissy, and so ready to sleep that every minute that passed waiting for that damn shuttle was filling me with rage. Well, maybe not rage, but at least the start of a temper tantrum that was quickly causing me to meltdown. I just wanted to get home to rest, and the stupid shuttle was a frustrating delay.

That was how I saw the ERA: like the shuttle that was dragging its feet and keeping me from my ultimate goal. The journey had taken so long and made us feel like we had perpetual jetlag. The last thing I wanted to do was stretch it out even further. My rational brain said this was a good idea. "The test could provide data that could greatly increase your chances of having a baby. You don't want to potentially waste another embryo, do you?" The other side of my brain was screaming like Veruca Salt. "But I want a baby now! And if I don't get the things I am after, I'm gooooing toooo scream!" I knew it was a good idea. I even knew we would ultimately end up choosing that route because it made sense. That didn't mean I had to be happy about it, though.

Chapter 67

As we were in the midst of another birth control cycle, all hell broke loose as COVID-19 crushed the world. I am not sure that I have to explain COVID because if you were above the age of eight in 2020 you should know all about it. In case this book takes off and becomes the definitive guide to dealing with infertility, is used as required reading material in schools, and goes on to reach a level of fame no book has ever reached before, thus allowing it to pass through generations that never experienced COVID, I will touch on it briefly.

We were with some friends in January (the same ones we were on our way to see when Brandi rolled herself out in the At Home parking lot) who were planning a trip to China in May. I had never heard of coronavirus before and didn't think much of it when they spoke about it potentially affecting their trip. The virus continued to move across the world and pick up steam, so I started to pay much closer attention. The full scope of the virus didn't hit me until the NBA canceled a game moments before tip-off. The announcer came on and a visual popped up on the jumbotron stating the game was canceled and to exit the arena. I immediately got on my phone to see what was going on. It didn't take long to understand that the NBA season was being postponed. Over the next few days, the 2020 NCAA Men's Basketball Tournament was canceled. I take two half days each year on the Thursday and Friday of the tournament, so for me, this news hit my core. I simply couldn't believe these major, billion-dollar events were being canceled.

The hits didn't stop there because after another week or so, life was canceled. Non-essential businesses were closed such as movie theaters, bars, restaurants, etc. Kids were sent home from school to continue learning electronically. People lost their jobs or were furloughed while almost every single event you could imagine was canceled. Life as we knew it had stopped. It got so bad that the government gave every working adult a check for $1,200 dollars. I don't mean people who lost their jobs got a check. I mean every single person who filed a tax return in the last few years. It was such a big stimulus package that they said, "Screw it. Ain't nobody got time to go through records and see who actually needs this money because they lost income." Nope. They sent it to everyone.

Since the world had stopped turning, one of our first thoughts was what might happen to treatment. Our clinic was doing what every single business was, taking it day by day. The news and state of the outbreak were ever-changing, sometimes almost by the hour. Would patients still be able to receive treatment? They didn't know. What if someone was in mid-cycle, would they be able to continue? They didn't know. Is a fertility clinic considered an essential business? They didn't know. My mind was pretty well made up that if COVID could cancel the NBA, then it was a no holds barred contest, and fertility clinics were about to be drop-kicked through a table.

Chapter 68

COVID claimed countless lives, the jobs of millions, and robbed humanity of so much joy. With such a horrendous event, it was a wonder that we, with the black cloud we lived under, came out so well. The stimulus check slid nicely into our medical fund for further treatment, neither of us lost our jobs, and it looked like we were going to be able to perform the ERA test just in the nick of time. We were hoping that we could at least get the test done before our clinic shut down because after the test was complete it would be another two full months before we could attempt another transfer.

It wouldn't be a day if the sun didn't rise and we didn't have issues, though. What should have been the most slam-dunk-worthy test was soon enveloped in uncertainty. No, COVID wasn't threatening our success, Brandi's uterine lining was the culprit this time. Any time Brandi had her lining measured it was always so plush, measuring twelve to sixteen millimeters. That's like Snuggle Bear plush. It was normally so thick, soft, and inviting for a prospective embryo, almost as if you were curling up in your favorite comfy blanket in front of a fire on a cold winter's day. Ah, so nice.

A few weeks into taking Estradiol, however, Brandi had a problem that was becoming annoyingly common. "I am having some spotting, and I don't know why," she told me with visible frustration that manifested itself in the form of rosy cheeks as the blood rushed to her face.

Son of a bitch. Here we go again. "Didn't you normally have spotting though before all of this?" was all I could say as it was becoming increasingly difficult to come up with new phrases to indicate concern.

Without hesitation, Brandi replied, "No, not really. I rarely used to spot mid-cycle. I only started doing that once I started all these fertility meds."

I was so tired of problems. I just wanted to find solutions. "Anything we can do about it?"

"Um, I'm not sure. I read some articles where Brazil nuts and pomegranate juice are supposed to help thicken it up."

The next day we ordered Brazil nuts and pomegranate juice through our grocery delivery service, and she started eating two nuts and drinking eight ounces of juice a day. The problem was the spotting didn't stop. Since the bleeding continued, the pomegranate juice intake was doubled. I asked if she would be increasing the nuts too and was told eating more than two Brazil nuts a day could be dangerous. The way she said it was as if she were taking ecstasy, and while two pills were fun, three could be deadly. The trip that three or more Brazil nuts would take her on could be more than she could come back from, I guess. She never said why, and I never asked.

By the time we reached the date of our appointment, we were nervous, to say the least. The twelve to sixteen millimeter lining with no medication had come naturally, so the prevailing thought was even with bleeding it still might be good. When the measurements were taken, the lining looked like Snuggle Bear had been carjacked and left for dead on the side of the road because it measured in at a measly six and a half millimeters. That was almost a third less than normal! *With medication!* The normally warm fire had been snuffed out and the comfy blanket was gone, leaving us to lie on the cold, hard ground.

The above is just a tad dramatic because while the clinic wanted her lining to measure at least seven millimeters, six and a half wasn't that far off. After conversing with our doctor, and some upset feelings on Brandi's end, we pushed our agenda and ended up being cleared to proceed with the ERA. That was a huge relief. As long the bleeding didn't intensify, and Brandi didn't take any bad trips on Brazil nuts, we were crossing our fingers that everything would work out.

Chapter 69

We were very pleased the appointment was still a go due to our passing grade, but we were concerned that we had received the equivalent of a "C" because we weren't "C" people. Simply passing left us unsettled. It was also hard to know exactly what this procedure would be like because not every woman seeking fertility treatment has this test. There were some accounts on various support pages, none of which had many encouraging things to say about the actual test, however. "Excruciating" and "incredibly intense pain" were some of the comments people left on message boards, so we knew this might be bad. Keep in mind too that no drugs for pain were provided, and the doctor was literally scooping a piece of her body out like she was a human pumpkin.

Our doctor and nurse came into the room to begin the procedure. A point that gets lost in this whole infertility battle is how comfortable you have to be with multiple people looking at your genitals. Men turn their heads and cough when they go for a checkup, but infertility is a beast of its own. During my portion of treatment, the doctor didn't just cup and feel around. No, he stared at and studied my testicles. Major veins were examined as if he were reading a map to determine which route would be the best to take for an upcoming trip.

For Brandi, the experience was awkward because she had always had a female doctor, and now, strange men were constantly staring at her and on occasion sticking what felt like their whole fist inside of her. Many people are not as comfortable with a member of the opposite sex being that closely involved with their private areas, so it is important to find a doctor that will help you stay at ease. A friend of ours had recently started her infertility journey and learned a painful lesson from the beginning about the awkwardness and invasiveness infertility can bring. Long story short, she was doing some at-home workouts, and one of the elastic bands she was pulling on snapped and lacerated her vagina. A few days later she had an appointment and not only had to expose her slashed genitals to the doctor but was also part of a training course in which residents got to take a peek. Talk about a rough start.

Awkward as it was, the doctor got out his miniature trowel and got to work. I had placed my hand on Brandi's body thinking she would grab it if the pain got to be too much. It wasn't hard to tell when the doctor first started scraping because it looked like the scene out of *The Exorcist*. Brandi went from a laid-back position to practically sitting straight up. While her head didn't spin, I thought it was moments away from popping off. The tears started and her whole body tensed up. Meanwhile, I looked like a terrible husband because she had a death grip on a hand, but instead of her supportive husband, Brandi had chosen to hold the nurse's hand. While Brandi cried profusely and was in gut-wrenching pain, I was left to touch her shoulder to keep her from jumping out of her skin.

While the pain was described as "super intense" and "the most extreme and painful pinching except it was coming from inside my body, so there was no way to make it stop", it was over almost as quickly as it had begun. She let out a thank-God-that's-over type "whew" and started to dry her tears with the tissue the nurse had handed her, thus taking away another job of her doting husband. I wish I could say that the worst part of it was seeing Brandi in so much pain and not being able to do anything about it, but that wouldn't be true. The worst part was when the doctor held up the sample he had collected like a child presenting something cool they had found in the back yard. I immediately went weak. It looked like a piece of bubblegum pressed on the bottom of a desk. I still wonder why he ever thought I would want to see that. Now, like so many other moments in our journey, it is etched in my mind forever.

Chapter 70

As we waited for the results of our test, fertility clinics around the country started closing. Infertility treatment is all about delays, but this delay was exceptionally difficult and frustrating for some couples because not only did it mean losing time, but it also meant losing money and emotional capital. As states started shutting businesses down, it didn't matter if you were one day away from transfer or in the middle of a stim cycle, you were done. No refund provided. Couples were left to take the next few months off to wait and then start back at the beginning.

I wasn't surprised that clinics were shutting down for a while, but the reason why had me a bit perplexed. Doctors explained to their patients that beyond the health and safety of people passing the virus to each other, there was inconclusive data regarding the effects on conceiving at that time. Could COVID reduce success rates or increase the rate of birth defects or miscarriages? It was all too new to know, and it wasn't seen as worth the risk.

I understood it was not worth the risk to some degree because treatment is very costly and anything that could negatively impact one's chances had to be taken into consideration. Hell, it may not have even been ethical for doctors to encourage patients to continue treatment with so many unknowns. I didn't know, but what I did know was that women who could conceive naturally weren't being told to hold off. In many cases, it became a running joke. Social media was abuzz with jokes about women becoming pregnant during quarantine because the thought was what else could you do when sheltering in place? Doing a puzzle or reading a book was an option, but people were obsessed with the idea of everyone constantly having sex and reproducing.

Jokes such as "I bet there is going to be a huge increase in the number of births come December," and "You must have *really* enjoyed quarantine," made the rounds. The main reason people in the olden days had tons of children (besides free labor and childcare, a lack of birth control, and an incredibly high mortality rate) was due to boredom. There was nothing else to do. With that in mind, I understood how those lamely repeated and worn-out jokes could be humorous but forgive me for forgetting to laugh. No one in the infertility community was laughing at those jokes because it was another reminder of the heartbreaking tax we owed for being infertile.

To the infertile community, it almost felt like a joke at our expense, like having a baby during COVID was done for sport. Brandi and I could Netflix and chill during quarantine, but we had no chance of making a baby. Painful truths like that stuck in my mind when a coworker informed me she was pregnant with her second child.

Seeming to forget who she was talking to, she said laughing, "We weren't even trying, but quarantine got to us. I guess we just got bored." The nonchalant nature and levity of the comment left me wounded.

"Congratulations," I said, trying to muster up my happiest thank-God-you-can't-see-my-face voice.

What do you say to someone who got pregnant because quarantine was boring, and they ran out of things to do? Must be nice to conceive a child accidentally because you finished your latest binge-worthy television show but before starting a new one you thought you might pound one out to bridge the gap between then and dinner. Must be nice indeed.

Chapter 71

After a few days, the results of our test were available. In a way, we hoped the test might find something wrong. That sounds strange but finding something wrong could provide answers as to why the initial transfer didn't work. If everything came back fine saying the timing was perfect, we wouldn't know what the issue was, but if we found we needed to transfer earlier or later, that would provide a bit of renewed hope.

Our results revealed that Brandi was twenty-four hours post-receptive. *What does that mean exactly, you ask? Well, in the world of regular fertility when everything works, not a damn thing.* The whole timing of conception and pregnancy just kind of adjusts to one's window and works itself out, but for couples facing infertility, being pre or post-receptive means everything. It meant that the timing of our whole protocol was wrong and could have been the reason behind our previous failed transfer. This was big news and a very helpful piece to our infertility puzzle.

Brandi tried to help me better understand by explaining what post-receptive meant because, in my mind, it meant that her body was able to accept the transfer after the five-day period, thus being post. Being a sports fan, this made perfect sense. The postgame comes after the game, so if we just make the transfer twenty-four hours after the usual time all would be well. That logic was completely backward. *Post* still meant after, but it came into play when the doctor took the initial uterine lining sample. Since the sample was taken on the fifth day and she was twenty-four hours post-receptive, it meant that by the time everything was done, it was twenty-four hours too late. The transfer needed to be done twenty-four hours earlier than day five, leaving day four as the optimal window.

Does that make sense? If not, reread the last two sentences and see if that helps. If you're still confused, Google it. If that is too much work, then let's just move forward. The results identified Brandi as a bit of a statistical freak. She shared a chart with me that documented 20,000 IVF cases in which around seventy-two percent of women who had completed an ERA were receptive, meaning on day five everything was ideal and went according to plan. The other twenty-eight percent were non-receptive. Within the twenty-eight percent of "why can't this just freaking work the way it's supposed to?" there was an eighty-five percent pre-receptive group and a twelve percent post-receptive group.

The test ultimately revealed that Brandi was in the subset of cases. To top it all off, she was actually in the subset of a subset of cases. I don't know what the bottom twelve percent of the bottom twenty-eight percent is, but I feel like around three percent is the right answer. *Feel free to check my math.* From me being in the one percent of men who have azoospermia to Brandi being in the three percent range of receptiveness, it was almost comical. Numbers can be cold and cruel, but fortunately, we had our new transfer window from the ERA test and were rearmed with hope.

Chapter 72

After obtaining our results from the ERA, our goal was to replicate that cycle exactly for our frozen embryo transfer (FET). Take birth control for a month and Estradiol for the second. The drugs started to take effect in the second month. I don't mean we could hear the sound of Brandi's uterine lining thickening and knew everything was working according to plan. I mean the drugs started to create cracks in Brandi's normally calm, stoic façade.

Things were already starting to break up a little during the mock transfer, so, to combat a possible emotional hurricane, I mentioned the possibility of getting another dog that summer. The death of our dog a year prior had been extremely difficult, especially for Brandi. Going through infertility was hard enough, but at least she had his unconditional love and constant cuddles. When he was gone, things just felt empty.

I am not a big fan of pets, but I recognized that this road may not be coming to an end soon and thought the idea of a new dog would put some very necessary pep back into her step by providing her with something to love and take care of. Selfishly, I knew that if a dog made her happier, then that happiness would trickle down to me. Plus, I wouldn't be the only one in the room on a bad day to bear the brunt of Brandi's emotions. In the end, it was going to be a win-win situation. A dog was deemed such an essential that instead of waiting until the summer, within three weeks of putting the bug in her ear, we had a puppy playing and running around the back yard. With COVID keeping us at home, a new pet provided the best distraction from quarantine and infertility.

With the new puppy, Brandi was better, but even without the puppy, she was far from awful or even unpleasant. Considering everything we had been through, Brandi had kept it together very well. Of course, when we encountered moments of disappointment and grief, she cried. She is human, but she wasn't prone to wailing or locking herself in the bedroom for days at a time. That was why I knew her minor meltdowns were just the drugs talking and decided to be as calm and comforting as possible. *Please don't infer I was always kind and comforting. I am simply stating I tried to be as much as possible. I'm no saint.*

The first such case of too many hormones in the body came when I was cleaning the gutters. Brandi was happy to watch me dispose of huge clumps of wet black leaves while she peacefully read her book and pet Calvin, our dog. I decided to remove a large stick from the roof while I was up there. In the process, however, the gutter snagged the stick and sent it crashing straight down on our bleeding heart. For all those non-plant parents, a bleeding heart is a leafy plant that has one or two branches that produce flowers that look like little hearts. Well, when the stick fell, it happened to land directly on the branch holding all the hearts.

"Why would you do that *JON*? Like what the hell?" Brandi yelped, as she abruptly sat up from her reclined position.

I was caught off guard by such a forceful response but immediately sought to defend myself from what was unintentional in my mind. "I didn't mean to. I was trying to throw it away from the house."

"You threw it straight down on it. I saw you, and now it's broken. Great. We can't have *anything* nice."

"I can fix it," I said, rushing off to find some zip ties in the garage.

With such an unsatisfactory response, tears began bubbling to the surface as she scolded, "That's dumb. The limb is BROKEN. The plant is DEAD."

"It's a perennial. It will grow back next year."

"I don't care about next year. It's dead now."

The rest of the gutters were cleaned in silence while Brandi cried to the point that she just couldn't bear to look at the man who had treated her plant so poorly that she went inside taking her dog and book with her.

The second instance included Calvin. *I knew he would be trouble.*

"Can you take Calvin out to potty? Make sure he pees and poops," Brandi instructed.

"Ok, I will," as I proceeded to take him outside, but after twenty minutes he wouldn't poop. After completing some outside tasks, I came back inside. "He peed but he wouldn't poop."

Using a tone that I instantly detected as trouble, she pressed, "Did you even try?"

"Yes, but I can't make him poop. I didn't watch him the whole time so he might have."

"That's the whole point of potty-training *Jon*. You have to watch him. You not watching him defeats the whole purpose," she said, bursting into tears.

"Oh, come on. Is it really that bad?" I was struggling to keep my temperature from rising.

"Yes, it's that bad Jon. Now I have to sit out here and watch him to make sure he poops when you were supposed to do it in the first place. Give me the leash."

Now I don't tell those two anecdotes to make Brandi look like some sort of lunatic or an emotionally off-the-rails person, but to simply illustrate that even some of the most emotionally well put together people are going to struggle. Infertility is incredibly difficult to manage, but when you add drugs, it can go sideways fast. Some women will handle medications better than others, but it is the job of the spouse to provide the best support possible and not to take the bait during silly arguments. I struggled mightily in that regard but got better as time went on. Just keep calm---and if worse comes to worst, get her a puppy.

Chapter 73

Before we could begin the second transfer, another measurement of the endometrial lining had to be taken. We were very nervous because, yet again, Brandi was experiencing bleeding mid-cycle, and it was a decent amount. To make matters worse, I wasn't allowed in the office for the appointment due to extra precautions stemming from COVID. While I waited in the car alone, I tried to focus on my breathing to keep calm, but the minutes passed with no word from inside. I thought for sure I would receive a text as soon as everything was good to go. That text didn't come, and I was too scared to text her.

Expecting a text and then not getting one is usually a sign of bad news. If someone has good news, they want to share it immediately, but bad news is a little harder to deliver. I just sat there looking at my phone over and over, trying to look out the window to keep my nerves in check, knowing that the longer everything went, the more conversations were happening, which meant alternative options were being discussed because this transfer was a no-go.

Luckily, the crisis was averted when Brandi came out and said all was good. They had measured her at six and a half millimeters and then again at eight. I was relieved that we could proceed with the transfer but was also coming down from an adrenaline rush. I was a bit peeved at being left in the dark for so long.

"Um, why didn't you text me when you were done?" I asked, clearly agitated, not caring if I started a spat.

Brandi hadn't acted this way on purpose and was slightly confused about my reaction. "I don't know. I was talking to the doctor and had to put my pants back on."

"And that means you didn't have time to say, 'All good' or 'Everything looks fine'? I am out here dying to know what the heck is going on in there."

"Sorry, I didn't think it was a big deal, and I knew I would see you in a couple minutes. *Calm down*. Everything looks fine," she said, putting her hand on my leg to steady my mood. Although the reassurance came quite late, I was at least pleased that it was reassurance backed by good news. We were still in business.

Chapter 74

The day of our second transfer had finally arrived. Many things had changed over those four months, from the weather heating up, to a global pandemic sweeping through the world, but at least we could rely on one undeniable truth. We were still infertile. Infertility was like a bad friend that we still hung out with but didn't quite know why. It was always there to knock us down when we were feeling good, borrow money with no intention of paying it back, be brutally blunt about our shortcomings, and always set us up for what seemed to be an epic prank just to laugh in our faces. Sometimes friendships run their course and relationships become toxic. Ours with infertility had definitely gone stale. We were hoping to start anew with our second transfer.

Once again, I was not allowed back into the procedure room due to COVID as only one patient was permitted to be in the entire office at one time. To be honest, I didn't plan on going to the second transfer appointment, but my physical presence was required. *No, not in the way you are thinking.* We already had the embryos, so my rust bucket of a penis wasn't required, but my signature was. We had to sign off stating that we were authorizing one embryo to be thawed for transfer.

Becoming combative with the policy in place, Brandi asked, "Why do they need your signature too? That's dumb."

I turned to look her in the eyes. "Well, believe it or not, this thing is half mine, so they really should have both of our permission."

Her features softened as she realized that I might be onto something. "Hmmm. I never thought of it that way because they were putting it into me, but I guess you're right. I guess it is half yours."

Damn straight it was. I worked super hard for that half, but that still wasn't the reason I had to drive up there. *Why didn't you just sign it and have her take it to the appointment? That seems like the easiest option as opposed to driving an hour to sit outside the office. Let me answer that question with a question of my own. How many of you have printers at home? Follow up question: how many of you have working printers at home? Exactly.* We have a printer, but there is no ink, no paper, and no CD-ROM slot on the laptop to download the necessary program. Also, if you have been keeping track, there is an invisible death-producing agent in the air, so stopping by our local Kinkos wasn't an option. Normally, I would have printed it at work like most people, but I was still working from home. I had to make the drive.

The drives to and from appointments were rather peculiar. I always saw them as a nice opportunity to talk to Brandi without interference from the outside world. After ten minutes of talking, however, the car would go silent. I would turn the radio on low to keep us from going bonkers but other than that, all was quiet. We normally have great conversations in the car but going to an appointment created such an uneasy feeling that it was hard to focus on much else. Our minds would drift to what could go wrong while we silently prayed nothing would.

The rides back were one of two extremes. The mood was either one of "let's go get ice cream and celebrate" or silence mixed with tears and disappointment. The silence on the bad news trips was deafening, but I knew it was best to let the silence take over, rather than try to find a bright side. Sometimes sad people don't want to be consoled; sometimes they just want to be sad.

We had good reason to believe this would be one of the good trips. The lining was within the suitable range and the act of inserting the embryo was straightforward. Brandi came out with the aforementioned paperwork and headed back in for the actual transfer. The whole event lasted maybe twenty minutes. We had a new picture of a tiny looking grain of rice that we decided to name Butterball.

In addition to our ultrasound picture, the doctor sent us home with more souvenirs: the picture of the embryo we transferred, and the instrument used to implant it. With the transfer complete and our goody bag in tow, we started home, but there were no McDonald's fries this time because last time they didn't work. My superstition was that if we didn't do unlucky things, the fate of this embryo might be different.

Chapter 75

With the timing of the second transfer and the global pandemic, a pregnancy would occur during ideal conditions. We calculated that if this transfer worked, the baby would be due around the end of January. Since Brandi worked a school calendar it would enable her to take off work and stay home with the baby through the end of July giving her almost six full months of maternity leave. Neither of us wanted to be a stay-at-home parent, but we were very interested in how we could, after hemorrhaging tens of thousands of dollars to create this baby, save money on childcare. Completing Brandi's maternity leave without losing much in wages would be a huge first step. After that, I would work two days a week from home while watching the baby for the next six months. That was our master plan to help "catch up" financially to other couples who didn't have to create human life through chemistry.

Additionally, the pandemic created a perfect cover for pregnancy. First off, it allowed Brandi to work from home, so when morning sickness kicked in or she had other feelings of being tired, it would all happen at home where the environment was much more controllable. There would be no running out of the room in the middle of a meeting to go upchuck. No falling asleep at her desk because fatigue was overtaking her body and mind. At home, if she wasn't feeling it, she could lie down for a bit and finish her work when she felt better.

Secondly, Brandi is a drinker. I don't mean she is an alcoholic by any stretch of the imagination, but sometimes the lure of a beer would be needed to get her to go places. Brandi hates trivia, but if I wanted her to go, all I would have to do was promise a beer or two, and she would be down. If I threw in an appetizer, she would beat me to the car. We had no idea how we were going to hide the fact that Brandi wasn't drinking when going out with friends was such an integral part of what we did. Enter COVID. We didn't leave the house, we hardly saw anyone, and if we did, people usually visited during the day when there wasn't as much pressure to pound a few. Hiding the fact that we weren't drinking during a virtual hangout was much easier than pretending to sip on a PBR tallboy out at the bar.

Was there concern regarding possible issues a pandemic could cause during pregnancy? Yes, absolutely. COVID was usually characterized by high fever, and fever during the first few months of pregnancy can be risky for the baby. We had been quarantining beforehand to not put the transfer at risk and knew that if the embryo took, we would have to be even more diligent. We were also concerned how COVID would affect the way we told people. While the concept of a grand surprise was gone, we still wanted to be able to tell our family and friends in a special way, but we didn't know when we would be able to see people. What about the gender reveal, baby shower, and people seeing the baby? We had waited a long time and wanted to do it all. At the end of the day, we knew that COVID would be a cloud over our pregnancy. A cloud in the sense that it provided us cover, but at the same time, it didn't let the sun through.

Chapter 76

First things first. We needed to get pregnant. On the fourth day after the transfer, Brandi had a moment of profuse bleeding. The feeling was utter terror. Could it be implantation bleeding? Who knew? It wasn't last time, so neither of us could rest easy. The only thing we could hope was that it didn't intensify and would quickly stop.

Since I was working at home, I finished my day and proceeded to the kitchen to get a snack. When we first started the IVF portion of our journey, Brandi purchased a felt board and easel with plastic white letters. This is a popular thing in the IVF world to help chronicle next steps and achievements. We used it sparingly because after so many setbacks it became a painful reminder of failed events. We used it when we first started, when we got her AMH results back, and after that to indicate what type of beer was in our keg for guests when they came over. While that wasn't the intended use, at least it was being used for something.

It was three weeks, four days since the transfer when I walked out of the office and saw the little easel propped up on the kitchen counter. That thing had been in the closet in between kegs, so I immediately knew something was amiss. Brandi was sitting at the table, secretly recording me, as I approached the sign that read, "It worked. You're going to be a dad. January 2021." Next to it was a pregnancy test.

"No. No, that can't be true," I said in disbelief, wrapping Brandi in a hug.

"Yes, it is," Brandi confirmed, fighting back tears.

Bringing it incredibly close to my face, I said in disbelief, "No…no…There's no way. How? I don't even see the line on this thing."

"Oh, it's there. I texted a friend to confirm, and she agrees there's a line there. My boobs have been sore, and this time just felt different. You know that bleeding I had a few days back? That must have been implantation bleeding." Brandi was beaming with joy as she shared the news. Her eyes and smile alternated from my face to the pregnancy test.

I still wasn't understanding the concept. "But there is no line."

Brandi let out a laugh. To her, the line was obvious because she had seen too many negative tests to count. She could recognize the faintest of lines from a mile away. "Yes, there is Jon. Look at it."

"Maybe," I said, twisting and turning it in every direction. "But it is very faint."

"That doesn't matter Jon. Any line at all means I am pregnant."

While we stood there embracing, I continued looking at the pregnancy test, still confused as to what I was seeing while concurrently thinking it couldn't be real. Had we really done it? Was this three-and-a-half-year nightmare really over? The look in her eyes told me it just might be. Of course, we still had a long way to go but this was a historic moment in our journey. I held her, released my doubt, and let joy and relief flood my mind and heart. We had done it. Finally! We were pregnant. That was something we had never said before, and it was finally real. I grabbed my best whiskey and had a glass to celebrate.

Maybe that wasn't the best thing to do in front of a newly pregnant person, but it was always the way I had intended to celebrate.

After accepting our new reality, I went downstairs to be alone for a while. While I would not win any awards for devout faith, one of the ways I like to experience my faith is through music. I love Catholic hymns and old-fashioned gospel music. The powerful feelings those old songs produce move me. I went downstairs and started playing some of my favorites. Maybe it was because some of the songs reminded me of loved ones lost, the fact that I believed God had finally listened to our prayers, or that the frustration and sadness of infertility had been building up inside of me, but as I listened to the music, tears began to roll down my cheeks. A few at first, and then I began to sob. I would get myself under control, then think about everything we had been through, and cry again. This created a sense of peace in my mind and soul that I hadn't experienced in a long time. The thankfulness and relief I felt couldn't be put into words, so instead, I just cried.

Chapter 77

Since false positives are a rare occurrence, we were feeling pretty good after the initial pregnancy test, but that didn't keep Brandi from taking multiple tests a day. She used cheap little strips in the morning and another strip, in addition to a more expensive early response one, a few hours later. Part of the reasoning was to see if the line changed in color and intensity based on the timing. The thought was the more concentrated the urine, the darker the line. Brandi also wanted to keep track of the tests and compare them day by day to see if the line continued to darken. The darker it got, the stronger the chance the pregnancy was viable.

The main reason, however, was that it was just plain fun and exciting to finally see a positive pregnancy test. Like a child who gets their first taste of sugar, we couldn't seem to get enough. We had never seen one before. Well, I guess that isn't technically true. We had seen one positive before, but Brandi's body hadn't created it, mine did. What makes those tests light up positive is hCG, so when I was taking shots to increase my sperm count, Brandi thought it would be cute to have me take a pregnancy test. I stuck the test into my Dixie cup dribbled with pee, and wham bam thank you, ma'am, I was pregnant.

When we were trying to get pregnant, we had read a few things about how to increase our chances of success. One book talked about cutting out plastics that contained BPA and how bad it was to heat food in plastic containers because toxins could seep into your food. In response to that, I threw out our plastic Tupperware and bought glass. I started paying better attention to water bottles and other products to see if they were BPA free. The seemingly silliest measure we took seriously was not touching receipts. There is something about the paper or ink that is not good to touch. Any time the cashier would try to hand Brandi a receipt she would either make me take it or have them put it in the bag. Several times, her refusal to take a receipt was met with odd glances.

Those tactics were the warm-up because, with a positive pregnancy test, it was time to kick it into full gear. We kept our superstition of receipts and added drinking smoothies every day with only organic fruit, taking more walks, and eating certain foods while avoiding others. Some of the information came from online, but more came from our new book collection. Brandi was so excited to finally purchase *What to Expect When You're Expecting*. How neat it was to find out that the pregnant woman on the front was the daughter of the woman who wrote the original book. Oh, joy!

If I thought for a second I was going to get out of my required reading list, then I had another thing coming. I was assigned two books for homework, the first of which I knew wasn't going to be my cup of tea. On the front cover was a cartoon couple embracing. The woman was hugging the man with her back to the reader while the man was holding a positive pregnancy test with blushing cheeks and a "Holy shit. Is this real?" look on his face. The book proceeded to tell a story about how the husband was on an all-night bender with some friends and didn't come home at a reasonable hour like he had originally told his wife. After waking up hungover, his wife essentially threw the pregnancy test in his lap and said they were going to have a baby.

This was a book written by a bro for bros, but I'm not your bro, bro. This was written for some guy named Craig who goes out one night, boinks a chick, and gets a call the next month saying, "You better get your shit together Craig because you're gonna be a dad. Sell your Camaro and get rid of your action figure collection. It's time to grow the eff up." The whole first part of the book focuses on stepping up, being a man, and helping your woman out. She needs you, so don't sit on your ass like a lazy bum. Get involved.

The book does provide some interesting, insightful, and helpful information, as it is wholly apparent to me that most men don't take the same path I did to get to that point in my life. For every one of me, there are four or more Craigs in this world. Now, to be a Craig, you don't have to be some piece of shit. You might be with a serious girlfriend, wife, or partner and still be caught off guard by the announcement of a pregnancy. Maybe it was very soon after marriage, you weren't trying, or you thought you were taking preventative measures, but even if everything seemed stable, it could have produced a red cheek, holy shit moment.

The problem was the book wasn't meant for someone like me, but there I was reading it. I had experienced almost four years of failure. I had Heath Ledger's Joker sized scars stretching along each of my testicles as a reminder of the physical and emotional pain. I had taken fertility drugs to increase my sperm count. I had seen my wife cry more than any man should over the first five years of marriage. At the end of the day, I am sure it is a fine book and will do a lot of expecting fathers a lot of good. Unfortunately, I'm just not your bro, bro.

Chapter 78

When we first found out we were pregnant it was three weeks, four days, and since we had only achieved my gag pregnancy up to that point, Brandi was still taking tests daily as the shock of it all hadn't quite worn off. When a "normal" woman gets pregnant she tends to take one or maybe two pregnancy tests at most because a positive test means a confirmed pregnancy. It is as basic as that. For a woman going through IVF, a positive test can be an oasis in a desert of failure and broken dreams, but after elation, the next feeling is fear because thoughts of "Could this just be a mirage?" start to develop. The fear is so real and so ubiquitous that a constant barrage of pregnancy tests feels like a requirement to help quell doubts.

A woman who has gone through IVF is usually wiser than a woman who has not. I don't mean more intelligent but at least, perhaps less ignorant. Someone who has gone through the process is usually knowledgeable of how long the road is and well aware of the fragility of the whole process. A woman who has never gone through IVF doesn't realize on her first pregnancy test what hurdles still need to be cleared. IVF women have usually lived in this world of fear for so long that they have armed themselves with more education, which in turn, creates more worry and dread. The non-IVF woman thinks, "Awesome. I'll start planning the baby shower," while the IVF woman prays, "I hope this is for real". An aspect that non-IVF women don't usually understand is that the early test could simply be an indication of a chemical pregnancy.

Chemical pregnancies are common but often happen so early in pregnancy that many women won't even know they've had one. An IVF woman will know, though. We knew we were pregnant at three weeks, four days. That was really early. A non-IVF woman might not even take a pregnancy test for another few weeks to check, and by that time, the signs of pregnancy may no longer be detectable on a test. A chemical pregnancy produces the hCG needed to show up on a pregnancy test but that is about it. We saw the positive tests and were now trying our best to get out of chemical pregnancy range which is about week five. Once a woman achieves this milestone, the threat of a chemical pregnancy is behind her.

The first checkpoint came with the beta test at a local lab two weeks after transfer. The last time Brandi had this test her hCG level was zero. A woman needs to see at least a twenty-five, but even that is extremely low. The acceptable range for a woman's hCG level at four weeks is so vast, it barely makes sense. It spans from the teens all the way up to seven thousand. That's a hell of a curve. The number we had hoped to see was something in at least the hundreds because even though the initial beta number didn't technically matter, why wouldn't we want a high first beta to help us feel a little safer? Although anything over twenty-five is considered pregnant, there is a gray area when betas are low, and the last place we wanted to be was stuck in "beta hell".

Our first beta test was ordered for a Thursday around four weeks of pregnancy, and the doctor was kind enough to make it a STAT order, meaning we could spend less time agonizing and would have the results by the end of the day. Brandi went to the blood draw and came back with an interesting story.

"So, you know how I got my blood drawn today?" Brandi asked as she walked in the door.

Since I was still focused on reading my book, I didn't fully listen or follow her question. "Huh? What are you talking about?"

Brandi was not to be deterred by my lack of focus. "I had my blood drawn to test my beta today. Where did you think I went?"

"Oh, I thought you went out for a Coke or something."

She pursed her lips together, unamused. "You don't listen. *Anyway*, I went to get my beta done and the lab assistant was really friendly and asked me why I was there. I explained it was a pregnancy test. She smiled and said, 'Oh how exciting' and stuff like that, and *then* spent the next few minutes telling me about her two miscarriages."

This incredible miscalculation of what one should say to a potentially pregnant woman captured my attention. "What the hell? Why would you say that (a) to anyone and (b) to someone getting a pregnancy test?"

Knowing her story had struck the right chord, Brandi's face lit up. "I know right? That's exactly what I thought. Really brought the mood down."

Despite that oh-so-fun experience at the blood draw, when the nurse called that afternoon with a number of 268, the relief felt palpable. We knew we were technically pregnant from the home tests, but having confirmatory blood work helped the pregnancy feel more "real". As excited as we were, we approached the news as we approached most things during treatment, with caution and tempered hope. Ultimately, a more important test would soon follow. After implantation, hCG can be detected and typically doubles every forty-eight to seventy-two hours. This doubling serves as a good indicator of a pregnancy's viability. We got to enjoy a bliss-filled forty-eight hours before attempting the next milestone---beta number two.

Remember how the first results were ordered STAT and conveniently received the same day? We had no such luck with the second beta. Due to COVID, many labs had reduced hours while simultaneously navigating an influx of COVID antibody tests. The test needed to be done on a Saturday, and our typical LabCorp location was closed. Brandi was left to find an alternative location to complete the necessary blood draws. Did I mention that these blood draws also happened to fall on Memorial Day weekend which complicated everything further? I mean, as you must know by now, timing *is* our forte.

Ultimately, we were informed STAT or not, the test results wouldn't be available until Monday, which felt like a double-edged sword. We had made plans for the weekend, and while it was nice to know that a phone call wouldn't be swooping in unexpectedly to ruin our day, spending the entire weekend without results was pure agony. When no call came Monday, I called Tuesday morning to press harder for results. Being the natural charmer I am, I had no problem getting the results emailed directly to us. Not sure why that hadn't been done earlier, but either way, we had what we wanted. Brandi didn't know if she could look, but I could and saw a number over the 536 we knew we needed---618.

Chapter 79

We had cleared two giant hurdles and were taking it day by day. Literally. Each day we woke up Brandi would inform me what day we were on. From week five and one day to week five and two days to week five and three days and so on it went. With each day that passed, the danger felt further away, and we started to enjoy the pregnancy. We started tracking how big the baby was from a poppy seed to a pea, revisiting some of our favorite baby names that had been shelved during this seemingly endless quest, and cleaning out the office that would soon transition to a nursery. We even started to let our minds drift to how we were going to tell our parents the good news. Father's Day weekend was at eight weeks and was the perfect date for several reasons. First, I was going to be a father, duh, and second, we could incorporate some sort of gift announcement without it being overwhelmingly obvious.

I clearly felt the shift in my mental state. I started to feel more content and excited that everything was coming together. We both expressed emotions of relief and exhaustion. There was an incredible weight lifted off our shoulders. I had always been very concerned about how much more money and emotional capital this endeavor was going to take and wondered if we would have enough. A few more doctor's appointments and hospital bills after the baby was born looked like chump change. Sure, it would still mean thousands of dollars, but we were going to have to spend that anyway. At least now, I wasn't going to cough up another possible $20,000 or more on top of it. As we saw a future not held hostage by endless worry and financial burdens, the world was looking good.

We had an appointment set for our first ultrasound to see the baby's heartbeat. We were both extremely nervous and there was a lot of concentrated breathing in the car. To make matters worse, I still wasn't allowed in the clinic, so Brandi had to experience that moment alone. I wanted to be in the room, good or bad, so the doctor permitted us to video chat as a compromise. To reduce background noise, I sat in the car with the windows rolled up, but even with that effort, it was very difficult to hear or see as the video was very choppy.

As the doctor started the ultrasound, I brought the phone closer to my face so I could hear while at the same time having to pull it back so I could see. Poor quality or not, I wasn't hearing anything. My PTSD from previous silent visits immediately made my stomach drop, and even in an air-conditioned car, I became incredibly hot and uncomfortable. The doctor finally began to speak, but I couldn't understand what he was saying. The first words I was able to make out were, "It could be a miscarriage."

My vision instantly blurred, and I had a hard time seeing the screen. At first, I thought maybe that wasn't what he said. I couldn't hear anything clearly up to that point so maybe he said something different, something positive like, "It certainly doesn't appear to be a miscarriage." I drew most of my clues from Brandi because she wasn't crying. If Brandi wasn't upset and melting down, then I had misheard. She was asking a few questions but overall didn't seem to be terribly upset. That was when it hit me though. This was the façade Brandi would apply when she was about to lose her shit but wanted to keep it all under control. She was a fraction of a second away from a tsunami of tears but believed if she could keep things technical, she could avoid the tears. She was stalling.

At the first "I'm so sorry" from the nurse, the floodgates opened. I was upset at the news and that I wasn't in the room to comfort her. I don't know if in my shell-shocked state, however, I would have been much use. In between the word "miscarriage" and the tears, the doctor found a moment to explain what he was seeing. The gestational sac was present and was measuring at six weeks but there was no fetal pole which is indicative of a viable pregnancy. In some cases, the gestational sac and placenta will continue to grow but the fetus will not grow with it. It stops developing at some point and begins to decline. Pregnancy symptoms like nausea, tiredness, and positive pregnancy tests continued because Brandi's body was still producing hCG. Everything was growing except the baby. Our experience was labeled as an anembryonic pregnancy (blighted ovum or empty sac).

A second ultrasound was recommended to confirm the findings of the first, but that was neither here nor there. The only thing I wanted was to have Brandi come out to the car so I could hold her hand while she cried. While Brandi was crying, the strangest thing happened to me. I didn't shed a tear. Yes, I was still shocked, but I didn't produce one tear. How could I be so unmoved?

I knew the answer. I was dead inside, and it wasn't the miscarriage that had done it to me. The repetition of pain and loss I had experienced over the last three and a half years had hollowed me out to a shell of myself to protect me from feeling this kind of pain. With infertility, most people reach a point where they don't allow themselves to feel pain because it is a survival mechanism akin to "if I don't let it in, it can't hurt me". I didn't feel I was actively barricading myself, but I had become numb to all things infertility. I've heard that if you throw a frog into boiling water, it will jump out, but if you put a frog in water and slowly increase it to a boil, the frog will die. The degrees of pain had increased moment by moment until I couldn't even feel the scald of a miscarriage.

Chapter 80

We added to our collection of silent drives with Brandi staring out the passenger side window while I stayed focused on the road before us. That silence continued at home while we both did the only thing we could at that time. Brandi cried, and I researched. I wanted to get as much information as possible and find any sliver of hope. After searching the phrase "blighted ovum at seven weeks" I found a copious number of threads discussing this very topic. Although I had never heard of a blighted ovum, it soon became apparent that it was a very common form of miscarriage. Around twenty-five percent of known pregnancies end in miscarriage and about seventy-five percent of miscarriages are due to a blighted ovum.

My main concern wasn't so much what a blighted ovum was because that didn't matter. Instead, I wanted to know whether there was any chance we were misdiagnosed. I soon stumbled on a treasure trove of message boards of women who had been diagnosed with a blighted ovum. A misdiagnosis could happen for several reasons: A tilted uterus (which Brandi had) can make it more difficult to locate the baby due to its position. The test could have been done too early; many women reported not being able to see the heartbeat until week eight, nine, ten, or even after. The type of ultrasound performed could have been suboptimal, although that wasn't the case because Brandi had a transvaginal ultrasound which is more capable of determining early pregnancy. The list went on from there. Of course, there were many more examples of women who were diagnosed and ultimately had a miscarriage, but the fact that there were so many that reported a misdiagnosis was highly encouraging.

Armed with fractional optimism, I still couldn't overcome the ultimate feeling that our fate was sealed. I shared some of my findings with Brandi to try and bolster her spirits slightly, but we both agreed not to get our hopes up. There should have been a heartbeat that day and there simply wasn't. The recurring theme of "we hadn't been lucky before, so why would we start now?" reared its ugly head. Whether we had experienced any luck along the way didn't matter in our depressive state. It was nearly impossible to not focus on the negatives at that moment.

On top of receiving the incredible sucker punch of knowing our dreams for our future child were dashed, we also had to discuss how we were going to proceed. We knew that step one was to continue the progesterone shots through the next ultrasound to ensure viability in the off chance that the initial ultrasound was incorrect.

After that, it got a little fuzzy. If and when the results confirmed a miscarriage, we could either have a dilation and curettage (D&C) or choose to miscarry naturally at home. The advantage of a D&C was that the physical aspect of a miscarriage would be over quickly and should result in total removal of all necessary tissue. There would be no wondering when the miscarriage was going to begin or how long it would last. Brandi was starting work again soon, so not knowing if everything would be resolved by then was a huge concern. The date would be set and while there might be some soreness that accompanies any medical procedure, a natural miscarriage wouldn't be any less painless. Additionally, it could also help decrease the emotional turmoil that a natural miscarriage produces. Brandi wouldn't have to suffer the possible traumatic effects of passing the accumulated tissue. The level of pain, discomfort, and mental stress the miscarriage could produce were unknown, but could be lessened through a D&C.

Upon investigation, however, there were several major drawbacks to a D&C. How much would it cost, and would insurance cover it? We were frightened and frankly, pissed off at the idea of paying thousands of dollars to miscarry. The hospitals were still dealing with patients from COVID, so they were the last place we wanted to go. Plus, we didn't want to spend the money on something as infuriating as a D&C. We already had so much hard-earned money squeezed out of us that another couple thousand dollars was unthinkable. Additionally, although most women have no lasting effects, some D&C's result in scar tissue which is not conducive to having children. Anything that was going to lessen our chances going forward had to be deeply examined.

The last negative we discussed sprung from a colleague of Brandi's, and while it may seem trivial to some, it can be quite damaging to others. A woman we knew had a D&C because of a miscarriage and received her bill coded as an abortion. Although seemingly benign on the surface, the word abortion to a woman who miscarried a very wanted pregnancy can be quite unsettling. For a woman who has undergone IVF and has fought for the chance to have a baby, a D&C coded as an abortion is a slap in the face. The mental anguish of having to pay a bill that implies a pregnancy was willingly terminated, when it was wanted more than anything, adds insult to injury. Once again, it may seem simple, but it was a hurt we were anxious to avoid.

If we weren't crazy about a D&C, our other option was to miscarry at home. The cons behind a natural miscarriage were some of the counter pros of a D&C. We had no idea when it would start or its duration. While work was starting up soon for Brandi, we also had a vacation planned before that. The thought of actively miscarrying during either was not welcomed. For me, I wanted to get everything over with as quickly as possible and move on to the next transfer. If it took Brandi weeks to miscarry, that was more time everything was being pushed back. I quickly refocused my desires to what was best for her mental and physical state because it was her body, even though I still craved speed. The anticipation and the act itself could be painful and dramatic. How much pain would be involved? Would it last for days, weeks? What if all the tissue didn't pass? Would we end up having a D&C anyway?

While deciding, we read that a surprising pro of a natural miscarriage could be how long it takes. When a woman goes with a D&C it is over in a matter of moments. That can be helpful for some who want to move on quickly, but it can have an adverse effect on the grieving process. A natural miscarriage is not as abrupt which can allow the woman and even the partner a chance to properly grieve and address the situation. Being a more immersive process, it provides a better chance to let go, say goodbye, and process feelings. While painful, experiencing a natural miscarriage can provide an overall sense of peace and closure.

We initially leaned towards a D&C because although we were afraid of the costs, the fear of a natural miscarriage was stronger. We had already faced so much and didn't know how we would hold up. The second ultrasound, set at eight weeks to confirm we were miscarrying, left us a few days to make this decision, so we compiled a list of questions regarding a D&C for our doctor. He had previously suggested this as the preferred route, but we needed to find out more about the logistics. Since nothing was one hundred percent confirmed, we knew we were jumping the gun, but then again, true to our motto, "we hadn't been lucky before, so why would we start now?"

Chapter 81

We spent the next week picking up the pieces of our lives, trying to keep everything as normal as possible. We felt one of the keys to surviving this ordeal was to keep the lines of communication open. We *had* to keep talking, keep sharing our thoughts and feelings. The last thing we wanted was for one of us to internalize the situation and keep everything to themselves. It wasn't a topic we wanted to discuss every day due to its raw nature, but we knew we had to check in on each other to make sure neither of us was getting sucked down into the riptide.

As we shared our thoughts, obviously sadness, disappointment, and frustration were the prevailing feelings but what was surprising was how calm and cool we were both acting about the entire thing. Here we were, having had our greatest desire ripped from us just when we were getting excited, and we weren't broken up about it. Let me repeat that we were sad and upset, but I cannot say we were distraught. That was slightly alarming.

I witnessed Brandi being more stoic than expected about the whole thing and encouraged her to express her emotions and cry when she needed to. While I wanted her to feel comfortable melting down if she needed to, I also praised her for handling the situation so well, with the caveat that crying and feeling pain wouldn't make her seem less brave or strong in my eyes. I was proud of her because of the body blows she continued to take and keep going. She could have shut it all down a long time before this miscarriage. She could have lashed out at me and blamed me for not having sperm and putting us in this situation to begin with, but she didn't do any of that. She even insisted we keep the movie night at our house for friends just two days after receiving the news.

Some people would say shutting down, lashing out, or being inconsolable are perfectly healthy and expected ways to deal with the loss of a baby. I agree whole-heartedly. Outside of a risky act or highly unhealthy activity, there is neither a right nor wrong way to deal with a miscarriage. We have all seen the spouse of a murder victim standing at a press conference appearing very calm and collected even in the face of her loved one meeting a tragic fate. The first thought of most is, she did it. I know for sure she killed him. Look at her. If my husband was dead, I would be a wreck. She isn't even crying. In some cases, intuition is true, but it doesn't apply in all situations. Everyone has different ways of coping with loss, and while I am no psychologist, the worst thing we can do is question others for how they are dealing with their situation.

I mentioned being dead inside earlier and that concept is precisely what was being portrayed in our home after our dream was dashed. If we had never experienced any form of fertility treatment or had suffered a miscarriage on our first transfer of IVF, it might have felt different, more powerful, but that wasn't where we were at that time. By that point, we had tried naturally for a year, ran in place for two years trying to figure me out, and then spent the last nine months fighting losing battles with IVF. Morale was low and the expectation that failure was the most logical outcome was high. Maybe that sounds negative, but losing affects the mind. Since we didn't expect much and wouldn't allow our hopes to grow too big, the bursting bubble didn't allow us to fall too far.

The biggest gripe we had with the miscarriage, other than the obvious, was that we couldn't just try again. I don't want to lessen the shock, pain, anguish, frustration, and devastation that a miscarriage brings to a couple who can conceive naturally, but I think it is worth pointing out that a couple going through IVF treatment experiences those same emotions while not being afforded the opportunity of "trying again for free" in the next month or two.

We started IVF in October of 2019 and had only transferred two embryos by the end of June. Eight months had passed, and we had only taken two swings at a baby. Sure, maybe that trend wouldn't continue, but we had no way of knowing. I never thought it would take that long to attempt two transfers when we first started. Additionally, a couple going through IVF must have money and the ability to take time off to attend appointments. These are luxuries naturally conceiving couples don't have to account for. A couple who can conceive naturally doesn't spend a month on birth control and pump their body full of hormones before trying again. They perform a free and ideally, enjoyable activity. An IVF couple must wait longer, spend more, and enjoy less, all the while being scared shitless.

Chapter 82

We spent the week between ultrasounds trapped in our traditional fog, somewhere between "This can't really be happening" and "It figures it would happen to us". Knowing we were going to miscarry was horrendous enough but even more so was the fact that we didn't know if we would ever find our way out of the never-ending fertility tunnel. The not knowing reached a fever pitch because we felt we had done everything right. We'd had a perfect embryo, implanted at the correct time, got pregnant, and yet there we were with nothing. Infertility isn't like a race. There is no predictable end that could help drive us towards the finish line. Every race has an ending point, yet we found ourselves running in circles with no clock to let us know when this hell would be over.

With no guarantees, would we ever be able to enjoy a pregnancy again? We had made it a little over seven weeks with plenty more in front of us that could go wrong. Assuming a third transfer worked, would there be much excitement over a positive pregnancy test? What about appointments? Would we ever feel safe at any point in the process? How could we? We had seen too much to ever feel comfortable again. It was going to take a baby in our arms to ever feel secure. We just had no idea how long that would take. It started to become more challenging to keep the dream alive. Although we didn't truly waver in our efforts to move forward, there was a sense of needing to stop for a minute, survey the damage, and confirm that proceeding was the best course of action. Regardless of what happened, the thrilling event of pregnancy, the thing we wanted more than anything, had been stripped of its luster and replaced by fear.

A second ultrasound was set to confirm the original diagnosis. Up to that point, we had not shared the news with anyone. There was still the possibility of a miracle, so we wanted to make sure before informing our families of the tragic news. I was allowed inside for the second ultrasound, most likely because the doctor knew there was no chance of a miracle.

The scan was short and much less dramatic than the first as it showed similar results. One noted change was that the gestational sac had shrunk closer to a five-week measurement meaning Brandi's body was recognizing that the pregnancy had failed. Only the progesterone shots were keeping the miscarriage from commencing. We found this to be mildly encouraging news as it meant Brandi would have less tissue to pass, thus making the whole ordeal slightly more manageable.

By the time we arrived at the second ultrasound, we had decided that a natural miscarriage would be best for us. Realizing that Brandi's body was naturally doing what it was supposed to made the decision easier. Our doctor agreed that a natural miscarriage would be an appropriate option in this situation and informed us that it would resemble a heavy period. Once Brandi stopped taking progesterone, the miscarriage would likely begin within a week or so. How long it would last and when we could start this whole process again was subject to debate. Monitoring would be required to ensure all the tissue passed, and then her body would have to self-regulate by having periods again. Ideally, we would be ready for another transfer within three or four months.

We had three major concerns leaving that appointment. What if Brandi didn't naturally pass all the tissue and we ended up having to proceed with a D&C after all? Beyond the cost and annoyance, it would be another black mark on our tally board of "Can't seem to get shit right the first time". Secondly, how long would this take? Maybe not so much the miscarriage itself but how long would it take for her to have her next period?

Naturally, being a man, I was very concerned about Brandi's reproductive system and wanted to exert as much control over her body as possible. *Some sarcasm there.* Unfortunately, in this case, my powers were deemed useless. I would have to wait while her body decided to get back into gear. Brandi being a self-proclaimed procrastinator made me uneasy that her body would subconsciously follow suit. Our tertiary reason for concern was how painful this would be. What physical pain would accompany this miscarriage and what type of mental and emotional scars might be left behind? No clue, but we were about to find out in a big way.

Chapter 83

If you would like the Disney version of a miscarriage then please know the princess finds out she isn't pregnant, the prince is sad, the princess wakes up one morning to see that everything is back to normal, and they both live happily forever. If you want that version, please skip ahead a few pages so you can continue to live in a world where elephants can fly, animals sing and dance, and evil is defeated in ninety-six minutes. If you want a real account of a miscarriage then continue reading, but know that it will be graphic, uncensored, and raw. Nothing will be presented in an overtly grotesque way for extreme shock value, but please know it will not be sugar-coated just like it wasn't sugar-coated for us. The idea that it would be anything close to a "heavy period" was a bit of a stretch. We were wholly unprepared for what came next, so if you have your big girl and boy pants on and think you can handle some carnage, then let's go.

To prepare for this "heavy period" Brandi purchased the largest pads ever made by mankind. I don't see a lot of maxi pads in my day-to-day routine, but these suckers were ginormous. They reminded me of my favorite SNL skit, "Oops! I Crapped My Pants". It is one of SNL's fake product ads in which an elderly couple purchases comically large diapers to keep them from embarrassing accidents. At one point the husband pours a gallon of tea into the diaper asking his wife to imagine it was a gallon of her feces to which the wife responds, "Oops! I Crapped My Pants sure can hold a lot of dung!" That is just how big these dudes were.

The event started with some warmup spotting a day or two after we stopped progesterone shots. "Just like the doctor said," we said. "Everything is moving along as planned." A few weeks of that didn't seem like it would be that bad. We knew it would be heavier as we progressed, but it didn't seem like anything the industrial-sized maxi-pad couldn't handle. Mostly light bleeding continued until we reached day seven. The Bible says on the seventh day all was good, and God rested. Well on *our* seventh day the gates of hell were let loose, and one of the most memorable days of my life occurred.

We were watching television when Brandi had to leave the room. I could sense her mind had drifted from the show as she started shifting around on the couch. "I have to go to the bathroom," she said.

"Can't we finish the show? There's like five minutes left," I asked, unsure of exactly what was occurring but sure it could wait until a natural break in the action.

"I think it's starting. When I went to the fridge for more water, I felt a whoosh." Brandi jumped up and ran to the bathroom as quickly as she could without taking full-length strides. It was more of a shuffle sprint than anything. After a few minutes she came back slightly on edge, "That was the worst one yet. The pad was almost soaked through. It was straight bright red blood when I wiped. There were some clots too."

"*Ok*…That's super gross! I'm not sure why you had to say that," I said, feeling I should have been insulated from the reality of what was happening.

Sheltering me was the furthest thing from her mind considering what she had just experienced. If she was going down, she was taking me with her. "Well, get used to it *Jon* because it happened, and there will probably be more." About twenty minutes passed and Brandi had to get up again. "Every time I move it squishes out of me. I feel it coming out!"

I didn't know what to do, so I continued sitting in my chair looking at my phone because I had no clue how to help or even how bad it was. After a few minutes passed, I found her in the guest bathroom with the door wide open. She was holding bloody toilet paper with something resting in the middle as if it were lounging in a hammock.

"Oh my God! What the hell is that?" I yelped, averting my gaze while attempting to erase that image from my mind.

"It's a clot," Brandi answered. Even though she was in the midst of trauma, she was able to keep a positive demeanor.

"Holy shit! That thing is huge. Why the hell would you show that to me? I can't unsee that. It looks like one of those California raisins."

"That is how big most of them have been that are falling out of me. I just keep wiping and the blood doesn't seem to stop."

Her response was matter of fact, but she didn't scold me for my over-the-top and potentially ill-placed joke. Most women would have had no room for humor at a time like this, but Brandi isn't like other women. Occasional bits of humor were welcomed to help calm her nerves.

I continued standing at the door looking in just enough to keep an eye on her but not well enough to be able to see what was going on. The possibility of seeing more clots was too high of a risk to take. The bleeding finally started to slow down, and Brandi decided she was going to bed. I was glad the ordeal was behind us and made myself a bowl of ice cream. I deserved a treat after all that hard work.

Since sports still didn't exist in the world of COVID, I watched the top one hundred dunks of the 2019-20 NBA season while enjoying a nice bowl of chocolate ice cream with little bits of marshmallows. I was watching DeAndre Jordan posterize some dude when Brandi called. "Get towels!" she exclaimed. "There's blood everywhere."

I threw my ice cream down and sprinted downstairs to get the old towels we used for rags and rushed back up with an armload. I found Brandi on the bedroom toilet crying and shaking with her lower half covered in blood. It looked like a scene straight out of the movie *Carrie*. It was horrendous. I gave her a towel to clean up, but she couldn't fully clean herself off because that involved getting up from the toilet. Any time she moved or attempted to move; more blood came roaring out.

The stream of blood was so consistent and strong that each swipe of toilet paper soaked right through to her hand. *Remember those commercial-grade maxi-pads?* Those might as well have been made of rice paper because over the course of an hour she had destroyed at least six. That was when we both started to grow concerned. Her concern was whether the toilet could handle all the toilet paper before it started to clog. To solve this, she started using a plastic Aldi bag to dispose of her used toilet paper instead of flushing every sixty seconds. The bag filled up quickly as the bleeding didn't slow down.

I started to become concerned when the bleeding didn't stop. Up to that point, I had been lying on the bed groaning and moaning in my most dramatic way at every trickle, gush, and plop I heard hitting the toilet. I was flat on my back on the bed whining and trying to focus on breathing in and breathing out. As I lay flat on my back, I stared up at the ceiling feeling my blood coursing through my veins almost exploding through my head. "I…I…I just can't," I whimpered.

Unsure what I could possibly be experiencing that would top her night, Brandi questioned, "You can't what?"

"Oh my God…oh my God…I just…I just can't…"

"Can't what? I am that one whose insides are filling up an Aldi bag right now."

"I know. I know…. but I just can't. Oh my God."

I did my best to fight off queasiness as I witnessed her lying on the ground on top of towels with one arm stretched out above her head. Beyond just feeling sick, her position was tactical. Brandi was trying to do whatever she could to keep the blood from coming out. If she stayed sideways, it stayed dammed up. Every time she got back up, however, it started up again. One time she got up too fast and a clot fell on the floor and splattered onto the wall.

It was at that moment I started Googling "hemorrhaging" and "when to go to the hospital for blood loss". She had been bleeding steadily for over an hour and everything I read indicated we might need to go to the emergency room soon. The resources I found said that a woman shouldn't be filling up more than one to two maxi pads an hour. I had seen her fill up a literal five and that didn't include what was residing in the Aldi bag or had been flushed down the toilet. We were way outside the "one to two an hour" range, so I started studying her for signs. She was still conscious. Check. Her lips weren't blue, and she still had color in her face. Check. When she did get up, before rushing to the toilet, she could stand. Check. Although she checked all of the boxes, we were still both concerned about her well-being.

"I am Googling 'hemorrhaging' and if we need to go to the hospital," I said, not considering the alarm this might produce.

The early humor had been fine, but this statement had clearly crossed a line. The panic set in as her eyebrows furrowed and she summoned what little strength remained to lift her head off the cold tile floor to look at me. "Oh my God. Why would you do that?"

"Because it looks like a war movie in here. You have lost a lot of blood. You're only supposed to be going through one or two pads an hour, not a six-pack. I'm concerned." I didn't want to concern her, but I needed to prepare her for this possibility.

She agreed that we might need to go to the hospital, and after another ten minutes of bleeding, she was ready. "Ok, maybe we should go. Put towels in the car. I don't want this getting all over my seats."

"Well, ok. We can, but let's talk about this for a minute. We should only go if you really think you need to. Do you feel ok?" I said in a role reversal.

"I don't know if it is the blood loss or if I am just scared. I feel a little weak, though."

"Yeah, that makes sense. My concern is it is a minimum of $1,000 to go to the ER and with COVID, a hospital isn't the best place to be right now. I just want to make sure before we go. If we have to, then we have to. I want to be sure."

"Yeah, that makes sense. Let's give it a few more minutes."

The fact that we live in a country where someone might be bleeding out and we have to consider the financial burden of an ER visit before seeking treatment is pathetic, but that is a conversation for another time. I was legitimately afraid something bad was going to happen but also paralyzed by fear that I was overreacting or misreading the situation. As I was putting towels in my passenger seat a thought of "Could I really lose my wife tonight?" brushed over me. I still wasn't at Defcon 1 because if I thought danger was imminent, I certainly would have paid the money and made the trip. Brandi's life is worth so much more than that, but the fact that it even had to be a question points to something bigger and more ridiculous.

To possibly bypass the ER, I began scouring the internet for foods that replenish blood. I understood it wouldn't be instantaneous but maybe it could help. Meats, nuts, leafy greens, and fruits topped the list, so I made a fruit smoothie with spinach and started force-feeding Brandi honey roasted peanuts. As I made her eat, she began feeling better leading us to believe that the fear of bleeding out was higher than the actual probability.

Fortunately, the bleeding started to taper off and become much more manageable. The food replenished energy lost and everything became much calmer. It was 1:00 a.m. I texted my boss that I would be a few hours late that morning. Thinking of work the next day, being sleep deprived, and clawing my way through *that* night seemed like too much. We took the last few clean towels we had left, laid them out on the bed just in case, and finally went to sleep. It had been the most vivid and alarming two hours of our lives and we were hoping it was all downhill from there. Could we complain though? It had just been a "heavy period" right?

Chapter 84

One day, when I was in kindergarten, we were told to bring our favorite teddy bear to class. My favorite stuffed animal at the time was Garfield, but since he was technically a cat and I was always one to follow rules, I decided I had better bring Pooh instead. Our classroom was made up of miniature tables surrounded by miniature seats, and on the back of each seat was a miniature satchel to hold our supplies and books. On this day we were instructed to put our teddy bears in our satchels while we went to recess as we didn't want to risk them running off!

Returning from recess, we found our room completely ransacked. Our miniature tables had supplies strewn across their surfaces, while some of our miniature chairs had been flipped over. Although we had taken the added precaution of placing our teddy bears in our protective satchels, the little S.O.B.'s had escaped. We looked and we looked, but we couldn't find them. Our only clue was paper bear paws on the floor, wall, and even the ceiling. Our teacher planted the seed in our mind that another bear must have taken our stuffed animals. Why a bear would steal other bears or how its footprints ended up on the ceiling was neither questioned nor answered, as we were too focused on recovering what had been stolen from us to care.

Around the school we tracked the pawprints from classroom to classroom, only to be informed that we had just missed the bear. We followed the tracks until we were outside in the park across the street where we saw our parents huddled around picnic tables. I spotted my dad who greeted me holding Pooh. It had been a ruse the entire time. While I wasn't pleased about being tricked, lied to, and having my adrenaline spiked, I was excited to see my dad and relieved Pooh hadn't been ripped to shreds by an angry paper bear.

After our miscarriage, I felt like that same terrified kindergartner who'd had his teddy bear stolen from him. This time, however, no definitive tracks were leading me to what had been stolen, and I couldn't count on my dad to be there, in the end, to make everything right. No, this empty, bottoming out feeling was ours to navigate alone.

For seven weeks, we had been allowed to dream. Dream about the future we had always wanted. I could imagine our little boy or girl playing with blocks on the living room floor or coming into our bedroom when they'd had a bad dream. I could see us going out for ice cream to celebrate an excellent report card or a big win in their favorite activity. I envisioned dropping them off at college, meeting their first serious boyfriend or girlfriend, wondering where all the time had gone, and being upset I hadn't treasured each day more fully. I could see those flashes of life, but those flashes had been only that. The flashes of my unborn child had been snuffed out before I got the chance to experience their full wonder.

I think every man or woman who has lost a child through miscarriage shares some of these same visions and thoughts. Would they have had my big blue eyes that Brandi so desperately wanted them to inherit? Would they have had her freckles and her laugh? I hoped they wouldn't get my temper but would be gifted with my sense of humor. I wanted them to have Brandi's intellect and passion for subjects of interest. What we want and what we get are not usually congruent in life. What I wanted, this child, was never to be. Never to be in my arms. Never to be in my life. Never to be forgotten.

Chapter 85

Now would be a good time to bring up a word that is not commonly associated with infertility: privilege. It may seem odd how the word privilege can even enter one's mind after having experienced a miscarriage, but it didn't take long for that word to continuously bounce around in our heads shortly after. Of course, that wasn't the first thing that popped into our minds. The first thing we felt was pain, sadness, and even some desperation surrounding the chance that things may never work out for us, but after all of that moved from the front of the line, privilege took front and center stage.

Even though we had experienced an incredibly traumatic event, we recognized how privileged we were to be in that position. I don't want to confuse luck with privilege, so let me be clear. We did consider ourselves very unlucky to have been one of the couples who experienced a miscarriage, but at the same time, we also felt lucky that we could even get pregnant. Some couples seeking fertility treatment never experience pregnancy. For some, the rope runs out right from the get-go caused by some medical roadblock that can't be cleared, while others spend years in infertility purgatory, never totally failing but never truly succeeding either. The fact that an embryo had implanted, we had seen a positive pregnancy test, and our beta increased according to schedule were all things to feel lucky about. There was reason for hope that the miscarriage may have been a fluke. We would have much preferred a viable pregnancy, but our spirits were not completely crushed.

That was the luck side of things, but I want to talk about privilege. Luck is fleeting. It comes and it goes. It can be good or bad, but privilege is more of a state of being. Once from privilege, always from privilege. Brandi and I were lucky enough to have the money to be able to afford treatment. Many infertile couples can't pursue treatment due to the fact there would be no possible way for them to pay for it. Others can start preliminary treatment, but reach their limit if results are not realized quickly. We had a much longer financial leash due to our station in life. We both had decent, well-paying jobs that allowed us to pursue treatment without much hesitation. Once again, we weren't rich because money was always a concern, but we could afford it. We could afford it because we were born into privilege.

We were both well cared for by our families, who were able to provide us with a good education, which allowed us to get decent, well-paying jobs. Sure, we worked hard through school and created and maintained a budget throughout fertility treatment so we could manage our money appropriately and set back enough to cover our expenses. We did all the right things that aren't a guarantee of someone who happens to come from privilege. Privilege doesn't mean everything works out in life, but it sure as hell makes things a lot easier. That fact cannot be ignored or taken for granted. At the end of the day, it was the position into which we were born and raised that set the stage for our ability to afford and pursue fertility treatment.

Chapter 86

Although we had made it through the initial night of terror, we were still not out of the woods regarding the miscarriage. Anyone with half a mind would have looked at that night and thought, no way in hell is something still up there, but we didn't know if everything had passed. Another screening was required along with repeated blood draws to test hCG levels to make sure they continued to fall back to zero.

Because of these variables, it was difficult to know exactly when we would be able to attempt our next transfer. Neither of us were ready at that exact moment, but at the same time, we didn't want to have to wait six months. We knew grieving the loss would be important, but we also didn't want to find ourselves in a sea of sorrow with nothing to look forward to either. The scan at the clinic helped put our minds at ease when it revealed everything had essentially been expelled and nothing additional would be required.

With that bullet dodged, we now had to wait for Brandi's hCG levels to fall below twenty-five before we could entertain the idea of another transfer. When labs normally draw blood for the purpose of testing hCG levels, it is to confirm a pregnancy. Obviously, not everyone is there for the same reason, so some level of tact and understanding is required.

"So, it looks like we are testing your hCG levels today. Is that correct?" the lab technician asked, looking at the paperwork in front of her.

"Yes, that's correct," Brandi replied in a defeated tone.

The woman didn't pick up on clues that would have informed her that Brandi was there for a not so joyous moment when she excitingly asked, "Oh! Do you think you might be?"

With a puzzled "are you serious right now?" face, Brandi replied, "No. I am here after a miscarriage."

While "Do you think you might be?" seems like a very innocuous question to someone who is pregnant, it is the last thing you should ask a woman who is in the final stages of a miscarriage. Unless that was the tech's first day, you'd think she had run into this situation before and had learned her lesson. If that is the case, how many times did she have to relearn it? If I were her, the first time someone responded like that, I would have been mortified and never uttered those words again.

Clearly, I am not this woman because she had a very short memory. A week later, Brandi found herself in the same lab for another blood draw. The technician drawing the blood was very compassionate and understanding regarding the situation, but on the way out they ran into the first tech who asked yet again, "Do you think you might be?" like it was some sort of sadistic catchphrase that must be repeated every time a woman comes into the lab.

Apparently, she caught daggers from the other tech, but it most likely did not deter her from living in her above the clouds mentality where she is oblivious to all things common sense. Going through something like a miscarriage is tough enough without fielding dumbass questions, but instead of Brandi firing back something like, "Do *you* think you might be an idiot?" she had to go with the tempered, non-norm shattering way of living in polite society and simply inform the woman once again she was there to confirm the completeness of a miscarriage. I am sure that response was met with an "oh that's too bad" as the tech floated away to the next patient unaware of what mental anguish she continued to dole out on a seemingly daily basis.

Chapter 87

Days passed as we came to grips with our new reality. We'd had a miscarriage and had lost our best shot at having a child. Never had we been so close and yet so far away. We were encouraged by the fact that Brandi could even get pregnant. It wasn't that we thought there was something wrong with her ability to conceive but in the back of our minds, the worry lingered. Each transfer has a decent chance of failure. That is just the simple nature of pregnancy. Our odds felt increased because we knew the exact time we needed to transfer, but just because the second embryo had implanted, it didn't provide any real guarantees of the third following suit.

In addition to that concern, Brandi had just had a miscarriage, and we didn't know why. We knew there was a good chance it was a chromosomal issue affecting the embryo, and we had just been unlucky. Yes, that was the theory, but it was only an educated guess. What if something more sinister had occurred in her body? Could it happen again? Multiple miscarriages happen, and I was scared to death of that prospect.

By the time we reached September and were ready for our last frozen transfer, the stakes were high, but there was a strange sense of calm. I take that back. It felt like calm, and looked like calm, but it wasn't calm. It was deadness with a coating of fear. The fear is what kept us on edge, but it was the deadness inside that presented itself as a twisted version of calm. How does one get excited about their third transfer and one-hundredth visit to a clinic for fertility treatment? How does one get excited when they know the potential result is devastating anguish and pain?

Sometimes I look at my dog who is slightly over one year old and think, he is going to die someday. I am going to have to watch that happen. I try to do something about it by lying with him more or playing with him to make sure I am not wasting these moments. I looked at transfers, especially after having a miscarriage, and thought, what if we have another miscarriage? Can I handle that? Can I go through another round of IVF, mentally, emotionally, and financially? The difference between my dog and our next transfer was I couldn't do anything about the here and now to help me feel better about the final outcome. I couldn't prep Brandi's body any further or make the uterine lining any more inviting to a prospective embryo. All I could do was keep moving forward.

The deadness I felt and the numbness my mind had accumulated over the years was my greatest weapon in blocking out future pain. In some ways, it was nice to have. In other ways, it has become the emotional scar I carry that keeps me from experiencing too much happiness or hope. As the years pass, I pray the emotional scarring subsides, but it could have a drastic impact on my future. This constant opening and prodding and poking over the last four years created a festering wound that can't heal until I hold a baby in my arms, or we decide to live childfree, not by choice.

This baggage made the third and final transfer rather surreal. There was no fear. There was also no excitement. It was akin to punching the clock at one's job. Just what you did at the start of the day. Punching a clock. That is what it had become. This highly scientific and delicate medical procedure designed to embed life into the woman I love with the hopes of having the baby we desired had turned into a routine: a robotic, uneventful, and almost mundane task meant only to kick start the process.

After the transfer, we both went about our business as if we hadn't just paid $3,000 to have a doctor impregnate Brandi with our potential first child. A week or so later, I am not even sure because that was how much it seemed to register, Brandi came into the room with a pregnancy test strip.

"I think there is a line there, but I can't quite tell," she said, handing me the strip and turning on a light.

"Yeah, I think I can see something there. It doesn't have to be strong at all so any line is a good sign. Cool. That's great," I responded.

Cool. That's what it had come to. My emotional response to finding out Brandi was pregnant was *cool.* Before anyone comes after me for my response, please note Brandi was not offended or upset by my lack of excitement. I was happy. Of course, I was, but at the same time, I couldn't reach my previous emotional highs. Brandi knew I was happy, but she had walked through fire too. A woman who had walked through fire didn't have the same emotional response either. There was no grand display to reveal the pregnancy. No cute little board with words proclaiming I was going to be a father. No rush to go out and get a good early detection pregnancy test. Brandi cared, but could she be blamed for her lack of enthusiasm the second go-around? Her body and mind had just gone through a torturous hell that might be set on repeat.

That was our new mental state. That was our new reality. We still had great days and many happy moments throughout the process but those were the "in-between" moments. Those moments occurred in between everything fertility related. When the fertility events commenced it was time to let the deadness take over and create that emotional shield. It was the only way we knew how.

Chapter 88

We knew we were pregnant again, and while on one hand, it felt like we were just checking a box on our way to impending doom, on the other hand, we knew what a huge step that had been. In many ways, this was it. This was our last embryo. One last chance at having this baby without sitting down for another life-altering conversation of whether we would want to proceed with another round of IVF.

When we started our IVF journey there had never been a doubt in our minds that we would at least go two full rounds, but as the weeks and months passed, that commitment was being called into question. We wanted to be parents but not at the expense of our mental health and future. While we were going through any form of fertility treatment, it became difficult to fully live. We were always holding back from experiences because we didn't know if we would need the money for treatment or if the timing would match up with our lives. We did our best to live normal lives, but sacrifices were made. Would we make those again to pursue something with no guarantee? That was a question we wanted to save for baby number two, not the here and now.

The next steps on our to-do list were avoiding a chemical pregnancy and getting positive results on Brandi's beta test. She passed that portion of the exam with flying colors when her initial reading was

562 and the follow-up a week later was 1,510. Since those numbers were significantly higher than before, we felt encouraged but unfortunately, not safe. Her beta had been high enough before, so we didn't know if the new numbers meant much.

A week or so before the dreaded seven-week ultrasound, where our hopes and dreams had been previously shattered, I started feeling ill. My mind still felt like it was numb, but my physical response indicated danger was ahead. I felt my whole system shut down and back up inside me. I was sick to my stomach and could feel a physical pit forming in my gut. It was as if my body was bracing for impact and wasn't going to let anything through until after the ultrasound. After sending strong signals that something wasn't right, my mind joined in the fight. I couldn't concentrate on work. I kept looking out the window, staring off into space. I would start typing an email, stop mid-sentence, and bore a hole into my computer screen, looking at nothing but thinking of everything. Mentally and physically, I kept bracing myself for the hit that was going to take me off my feet; waiting for that moment Brandi would walk through the door and tell me she had bleeding that morning which would cause my stomach to drop through the floor. The paranoia was consuming me, making me miserable.

The appointment was set for early afternoon, which meant I had to somehow focus on my job while alarm bells were sounding in my head. Maybe it was better that way. I don't remember most of that morning because my mind was being ripped in two directions.

There had been more silence in our house the last few days as each of us sought to prepare in our own way. I emerged from the office, grabbed my keys and wallet, and sat down in the recliner, waiting for her to join me in the living room. She passed through the kitchen to fill up her pink hydro flask and grabbed a banana for the road.

My tone was that of going to a funeral. I asked a question that no one wanted to answer. "Are you ready?"

"Yep," was all I got as she looked at me with an expression of "let's get this over with". There was little room for excitement at that moment.

The thirty-eight-minute drive went by in silence with each of us staring straight ahead. I made the familiar left turn towards the CVS we had passed dozens of times before. Another left led us onto a small and narrow road that wound around a hotel, several businesses, and an elderly care facility as the interstate raged to our left. As I neared the first of two yellow speed bumps, I slowed to a crawl to avoid any disruption in the pensive mood that a fast approach would have caused.

After gliding over the bumps, we arrived at the parking lot. My superstition had always been to park in a new spot if that last visit had been bad news and park in the same spot if the visit had revealed good news. Normally, I was finding a new spot, and that day was no different. I decided against parking in the direction that faced what had become my house of horrors and instead chose to face the interstate.

It was still the fertility clinic's policy to only allow one patient in at a time alone. This policy terrified Brandi so much that she called and asked for leniency. The pain of the last visit and having to face the devastating news of a miscarriage by herself was more than she felt she could handle a second time. The clinic heard and understood her fears but was unwilling to make an exception. It was a very annoying decision to us, especially because I had previously been allowed in the room last time to confirm the results of our miscarriage. As much as we didn't like the stance, we understood they needed to reduce their exposure points to COVID because the clinic had one main nurse and doctor. If one of those two went down, the whole operation would tailspin.

On pins and needles, we waited for the call from the main office. I started to panic. I would inhale a shaky breath and try to steady myself on the exhale. My body started to twitch as I found the car to be an incredibly uncomfortable place. Twisting and turning, I continued the hunt for a comfortable position, but none was found. My actions were not helping Brandi's anxiety, but someone having an anxiety attack can't be called on by another to calm them down.

The call came, and as Brandi was gathering her purse to go inside, I gathered all the strength I had left and said, "Hey. No matter what happens today, know that we will get through this and tackle it together like we always do."

"I know we will," she said, looking into my eyes. "I don't know why, but I feel good about this one. I really do. Let's hope for the best."

The car soon felt like a coffin. There was no air and no escape. It was getting warm, and I felt like I couldn't breathe as I continued to shift and squirm in my seat. I didn't dare open a window because I had struggled to hear the last video call. More importantly, I didn't want the person parked two spots next to me overhearing my life. This was our moment, not theirs. They hadn't put in the blood, sweat, and tears and didn't deserve to take part in even the smallest of portions. Would the couple in the car next to me have been able to hear anything with their windows rolled up? Absolutely not, but I wasn't going to let anyone else in at this pivotal moment.

My phone buzzed in my hand as I pressed the green button revealing Brandi's face covered mostly by a mask. Since we were on a video call, it felt like someone should say something but neither of us had anything to say. Instead, I thought about the video Brandi had shown me a few weeks ago of a seven-week ultrasound, so I would know what to expect. The last ultrasound had revealed a black empty hole where we should have seen a flickering silver light indicating a baby's heartbeat. I prayed with all my might that we would see that silver flash.

We continued saying mindless things to each other to pass the time when the doctor and nurse came into the room. The customary "hello" and "how are you feeling?" were exchanged, but I could only focus on the fact that this was it. The fate of the rest of our lives rested on the results of a five second ultrasound. Five seconds was all it was going to take for us to know whether a baby was present. Five seconds was probably on the long end for our doctor because he would know within three and the other two would be us reading his reaction. He inserted the transvaginal wand and time stopped.

When I was eleven years old, I went to school like I did every day, but one day stands out in my mind. We always left very early before the sun came up as my mom had to be at work across town. I was the kid that got there before the janitor arrived to open the door, while at the same time, being one of the last kids to be picked up after school. That morning I remember the song on the radio being "Sultans of Swing". I stared at the glowing dials on the radio as I listened to the words, "They don't give a damn about any trumpet playin' band," which were my favorite because being eleven, the word "damn" was taboo but made me feel something.

The day went by uneventfully, and my mom arrived to take me home. The answering machine had its familiar red blinking light, but the news it held from my uncle was not good. I remember hearing the words "heart attack" and "died". I immediately rushed to the living room couch and buried my face in a pillow. My grandpa had been the one that watched me when I didn't have school, but my parents had to work. I remember being dropped off while *Good Morning America* was on TV and him stepping outside for an early morning cigarette while sipping coffee from his plain brown mug. Our tradition was to go to McDonald's for a Happy Meal and to watch movies while he fell asleep in the chair and snored so loudly that I could hear nothing else.

He and my grandma were at almost every sporting event where he encouraged me to take more hook shots after I had displayed late-game heroics with one. "Show them it's not a fluke," he said, even though we both knew it was most likely just that. He was the one who took me to Home Depot for their building days where we built a birdhouse and toolbox together. He was my grandpa, and I loved him dearly. That day, however, was one of those days with a clear before and after. Everyone has those moments in their life where there is no going back to the time you just left: a change in life's direction.

Sitting in the car, waiting for an image to appear on the ultrasound screen was one of those moments that would mark a before and after in both our lives. I saw shades of black and grey swirling around, changing directions as he maneuvered the wand into position. My mind raced, and my palms grew sweaty as I pushed on the floorboard to steady myself. My phone was pressed up against my face as if drawing it closer would expedite the process. Another swish and... wait. What was that? Did I just see something, a little silver flicker dancing on the screen? I wasn't sure what it was because it was so small. I only knew I hadn't seen it last time.

My blood was pumping, begging the doctor to say something, anything. The first words were not his, however, when Brandi asked with an audible lump in her throat, "Is that the heartbeat?" Her hesitant question was waited on with great anticipation, as I had no idea what I was looking at but praying she was right. The doctor confirmed that what we were seeing was indeed the baby we had desperately waited to see for four years. At that moment, I felt my whole body relax, like steam being released from a pressure cooker. I was joyous and excited, but at that moment, mostly relieved. I knew the journey ahead was still long, but we were pregnant. We watched a strong 143 bpm heartbeat rhythmically chug along on the monitor and were amazed at how fragile and amazing life is.

As Brandi emerged from the clinic, both of us wanted to feel more happiness than we did initially. It was akin to witnessing an unbelievable last-second win in sports, where fans are left in a state of almost shock, pinching themselves, trying to make sense of exactly what happened. We were in shock. After four years of constant wishing and hoping, it finally felt real. She showed me the three ultrasound pictures with our tiny silver speck peeking through the darkness. I held it in my hand and all I could do was smile. We *finally* had good news.

Chapter 89

Emotionally going from zero to sixty, our minds were buzzing on the car ride home. The excitement was palpable as Brandi held physical representations of our baby in her hand and replayed the video over and over of our silver flash's heartbeat steadily thumping. Although I was driving seventy miles an hour, weaving in and out of traffic, with bright eyes, she turned the phone towards me encouraging me to watch the video. "Look at your baby Jon. Look at how little they are. I just love listening to the heartbeat."

It was an incredible feeling knowing we had made it to this point. As excitement filled the car, the lingering sense of worry that we still weren't out of the woods was thick. *You're probably saying, "Just be happy, man. You're finally pregnant."* We were absolutely thrilled, but we had also been inured to infertility for so long that it made it hard to reach out and hold on to joy.

The feeling reminded me of an experiment in which psychologists placed a carnivorous fish in a tank with smaller fish, separated by glass. The carnivorous fish kept trying to break the glass divider down by ramming into it but couldn't get through to the fish on the other side. After enough unsuccessful attempts, the barrier was removed, but the carnivorous fish made no attempt to eat the smaller fish even though they were now easily accessible. This is called Pike syndrome, and although our situation wasn't identical, it contained parallels. We had been trying to break through an impregnable wall for four years. Suddenly, the obstacle had been removed, but we had been so conditioned to stay on our side of sorrow that it proved difficult moving towards the acceptance of happiness. We had grown so accustomed to fear and worry that it was difficult to accept anything else.

Our goal was to make it to the next milestone which would be the nine-week ultrasound. In all actuality, each day that passed marked a milestone. Brandi would research what the rate of miscarriage was at seven weeks two days, seven weeks three days, seven weeks four days. She did this every day to help recondition her mind that things might be ok. As the percent chance began to decrease with each passing day, a blanket of security began to envelop her. While I wasn't checking Google with the same fervor, I was hoping and praying that we would escape each day without incident. Each day that passed with no news was good news in my mind.

Treading through the perilous waters of each new day was excruciatingly slow and painful, but after what felt like the longest two weeks of our lives, we were ready for the nine-week ultrasound. Other than the shots we had been continuing to plunge into Brandi's backside, there was no real indication that she was pregnant. She hardly had any symptoms and naturally, the baby was too small to feel. We had nothing to go off except our last ultrasound. We were in the dark and believed the next one could go either way. Worry turned into dread when Brandi called the morning of the appointment.

As my phone silently lit up, I stepped outside to answer, when I heard her quivering voice. "Jon?" she said with bated breath before bursting out, "I had bleeding today, and it was quite a bit. Like, it covered quite a lot of the toilet paper and was light pink. I'm freaking out. I had to call off work because I just can't right now."

I felt my body go limp and my throat started to close. "How much blood are we talking about exactly?"

"Umm...quite a bit. Can I send you a picture and you tell me what you think?" I opened the text to reveal an image of a strip of toilet paper stained with pink blood. "I called the clinic and sent them the picture. They said we could come in an hour earlier to help put my mind at ease. Only good thing is we have the appointment in a few hours, or I don't know what I would do."

The problem was I didn't know what to do either. I told myself it was probably nothing. Many women experience bleeding during early pregnancy and nothing comes of it. The Google results of "blood at nine weeks pregnant" were calming as they tended to back my notions. I tried to convince myself that this was no big deal, while at the same time I chided myself for getting my hopes up. This is why you can't let your guard down and feel safe. You started to feel good about the whole thing and now look. The next three hours were some of the longest hours of our lives.

Chapter 90

As we arrived at the clinic, I headed for our lucky spot, but it was unfortunately taken by another patient. Not parking there made me feel uneasy, but my superstitious brain hoped parking on the same side, facing the interstate would be lucky enough. Every appointment at that point felt like *Groundhog Day*. Get in the car, nervous as hell. Drive to the clinic, nervous as hell. Wait in the parking lot to be called in, nervous as hell. Brace for impact, nervous as hell. We had been in the same vicious cycle for so long, stuck on repeat. The last time we had been there, however, the spell had been broken. We hadn't left with devastating news and been sent home to repeat the horrid process. Maybe, just maybe, it was February third and things were going to be different.

By this point, you know what I was feeling. We've been here enough. Blood pumping. Bowels churning. Complete discomfort. I was holding my phone in a shaking hand, growing frustrated Brandi hadn't called yet, wondering what was taking so damn long. Finally, she called, and then I grew frustrated with the doctor wondering what was taking *him* so damn long. I was scared and internally lashing out at everyone I could think of because I didn't know how else to regulate my emotions.

Brandi briefly spoke to the doctor and nurse about her bleeding. The only way to find out more was to proceed with the ultrasound. I was in no mood to mess around. Just get in there, find the baby, and let me hear the heartbeat. Let's not have any issues locating anything, no hesitant speech, and absolutely no silence. I didn't come this far and go through this much to lose this baby now. Fortunately, I didn't have to wait long to see a much larger image of our silver baby happily chilling on the screen. Even better is that babies' hearts are so large and prominent at that stage, it made it easy to identify a beating heart. The doctor confirmed what we saw by displaying the heartbeat pumping in perfect rhythm. What had caused the bleeding? No one seemed to know. Nothing visible had been found during the ultrasound and if it didn't continue, there was no major cause for alarm. Baby and mother were doing well, and that was all that mattered.

Normally, we would have moved on from our fertility clinic after the nine-week ultrasound, but just to be safe, the doctor suggested we come in for one more visit at week ten. He wasn't overly concerned about the bleeding, but one more check wouldn't hurt. We were in total favor of this as it would continue to provide peace of mind, and any chance to see and obtain further confirmation of our baby's well-being was welcomed. The clinic was also interested in seeing us again because they normally didn't get to see babies at ten weeks. It would be a real treat for them as well.

There was no more bleeding between weeks nine and ten, and our confidence was growing. We could finally stretch our legs and feel secure that things were moving in the right direction. The feelings of fear and worry about what might go wrong were still present but were decreasing with each passing day. We finally permitted ourselves to dream again. Our dreams became even more vivid after we did a sneak peek gender reveal around eight and a half weeks. The test yielded a ninety-nine percent accuracy rate, and we weren't going to be one of those couples that could wait until the birth to find out the gender. Some couples who have gone through infertility seek to keep the gender unknown until birth because the whole process has taken the surprise out of everything. We were the opposite. Every element of surprise had been washed away, so why stop now? We had to know.

A week or so after taking the blood test, our results came back in an email. We had both been obsessively checking our emails, but my timing was better because I saw it first. I clicked on the email, and immediately, colored balloons and streamers started shooting across the page. It said congratulations, revealing the gender.

"So, we got the gender email," I said tepidly because I knew I was going to be in trouble in about thirty seconds.

Brandi lit up with an immediate smile, excitedly expectant to share the news together. "Oh, we did? I have been checking it all day! Come over here so we can look together."

"Ok…so, about that." I explained to her that I had opened the email and had seen the gender.

Her face took a one-eighty. "Why would you do that? We were supposed to open the email together."

Looking for a way out I said, "I thought I was going to have to open the email and click on something. I didn't know it was going to prompt a celebration just by opening it. I'm sorry."

Brandi was so excited about the prospect of learning what the gender was that it didn't bother her too much that I had ruined the last possible surprise. "Well, what is it?!" she exclaimed. "I think it's a boy."

I walked over to her with my phone and opened the email. Immediately, blue balloons and streamers started shooting across the page and it said congratulations, revealing we were having a boy. We were ecstatic and like most couples, we didn't care what the gender was as long as they were healthy. That was all we really wanted.

Chapter 91

The day of the ten-week ultrasound arrived and the mood was completely different than previous visits. We were ebullient and actually looking forward to the ultrasound. We had seen a happy healthy baby a week ago and were armed with the knowledge we would be looking at our son. Success breeds confidence. While our minds had been altered and shaped by the trials of our journey, we were starting to believe having a baby was possible. The last few visits had created a new outlook on life for us. The last four years were starting to come into focus, and we could see an end in sight.

I watched Brandi in the rearview mirror head into the clinic and turned the volume up on my phone to wait for her video call. She popped up on the screen, and the ultrasound began. What we saw was truly remarkable. A week ago, our baby looked like an amorphous blob, but just one week later he looked human; well, if humans had overly sized heads with short, stout little bodies and short, stout little hands. Maybe he looked less like a human and more like a gummy bear. He was squirming around, wiggling his little hands and little feet. We got to record his movements and it may be one of the cutest videos I have ever seen. Witnessing what we had struggled for, worked so hard for, and gave up so much for, now being in front of us, moving around without a care in the world, was extraordinary.

The nurse asked if they could have a copy of the video for the website since they didn't get to see that many ten-week babies. We readily agreed to share the video, thus commencing our first proud refrigerator moment in what would be many for our little boy, whom we had named Lucky #3. It was a strange moment in our journey; a crossroads marking the beginning of one chapter of our lives and ending another. We knew that if we wanted another child we would have to come back and start the process again, but that was in the future. The here and now of it was we were leaving a world in which infertility had ruled our lives, thoughts, and actions. Graduating from our clinic meant we could move past that part of our lives and start focusing on the future with our child.

COVID be damned as the nurse gave Brandi a hug to celebrate. She and the doctor had been on this journey with us for a year, so they took pride in our success. Brandi promised her that we would bring our baby by to say hello and to thank them for all they did. Without their help, our future would look incredibly different. She paid our last bill and exited the doors of the clinic looking down at our new ultrasound pictures with a grin on her face that stretched from ear to ear. I hugged her, and we sat there for a moment in silence, looking at the pictures in awe. We replayed the video of our little gummy bear bouncing around, sharing a truly special moment. As we headed home, I turned to look at the clinic one last time in the rearview mirror, hoping that was exactly where it stayed.

Epilogue

I started writing our story of infertility a little over two years into the process, having no idea what the end result would be. Writing while going through four years of infertility was incredibly difficult at times. Recounting emotionally scarring moments and capturing their true essence on paper shortly after they had occurred created a unique challenge, but compiling these events and feelings proved to be quite therapeutic. After most sections, I would bring Brandi into the room and read what I had written. It allowed us to feel the moment again, discuss our thoughts and emotions (some of which were much stronger when recollecting versus when we were going through it), and begin to heal.

The ending to our story is a happy one. We went through IVF and got the baby we so desperately wanted. At some point, I made a conscious decision to conclude our story after the third embryo, with or without success. To continue until we had achieved success wouldn't have been respectful to all the couples who go through infertility but do not achieve their ultimate goal. Infertility treatment ends poorly for so many people. There isn't always a pretty bow that gets tied around it as many pour their hearts and souls into a process that has no intention of allowing them to taste success. Infertility takes. It doesn't always give back.

Some would say we "beat infertility", but there is no such thing. If we want to have a second child, we still have to go back to our clinic, go through stims, transfers, and perhaps more failure. We are still infertile. Couples can't really "beat infertility", and to imply they can, does a great disservice to those who can't conceive through the process. It implies that the couple didn't try hard enough.

From the outside looking in, it is easy to say, "Just go another round," or "Don't give up. If you keep trying, it will work out." If a couple decides they have spent enough time, money, and emotional capital and chooses to be done, have they quit? Are they quitters? Brandi and I spent four years and over $40,000 to have a baby: if our last transfer hadn't worked and we made the conscious choice to walk away because the all-consuming nature of infertility had taken a terrible toll, would we have been quitters? Draw your own conclusion, but I say, hell no. We tried. We gave it everything we had. Just because we had enough money in the bank to go another round or mentally felt we might be prepared to tackle it again didn't mean it was a wise investment. Every round of treatment is a gamble, not destined to always pay off. Protecting our mental well-being, financial health, and taking back our lives would have been worthy enough reasons to walk away and live childfree, not by choice.

Living childfree, not by choice, would have been our preferred path if IVF ultimately provided to be fruitless. Our goal was never to just have a child, it was to have a biological child, and if that wasn't going to happen then we were prepared to be done. Everyone has their own line in the sand. What each couple can and is willing to do is their business because it is their lives. Some couples will seek alternative options if IVF fails. Some will give it everything they have and believe that if they don't exhaust every last option, they have failed. Others realize they can't and won't give everything they have to this process and will find happiness in something else.

At the end of the day, infertility isn't something to be beaten; it's something one lives with forever in most cases. Having a baby is a triumphant moment but the battle against infertility rages. Instead of creating a position where one must win or lose to infertility, we need to create healthy dialogue and a more mainstream approach to discussing the issues, so it becomes less black and white. Going through treatment is tough. Feeling judged or pressured by people outside the community or even people within it makes it all the more difficult. If someone chooses to walk away from infertility without a baby, don't take the approach that they gave up or decided to quit. Understand they gave what they were willing to give and felt they had to be done. It was their road to walk, and they had simply reached the end.

Printed in Great Britain
by Amazon